THE SHORT HISTORY OF BRITISH BATTLES

From Hastings to Trafalgar

Paul Davies

Amazon Publishing

To my family and friends.

"Firstly you must always implicitly obey orders, without attempting to form any opinion of your own regarding their propriety. Secondly, you must consider every man your enemy who speaks ill of your king; and thirdly you must hate a Frenchman as you hate the devil."

HORATIO NELSON

CONTENTS

HASTINGS

Beginning of Norman Rule

1066

The Battle of Hastings, which was fought on 14th October 1066, was one of the most important events in English history. By his victory William, Duke of Normandy, was able to begin subjugating England to Norman rule, and establishing feudalism.

William had planned his invasion six months previously but adverse winds had delayed the embarkation which had been timed for late summer. Fortunately for him, a large Scandinavian army had landed in the north of England, and was ravaging the countryside when his cross-Channel journey became possible. Harold, the English king, hearing of the northern threat promptly rushed north. At Stamford Bridge, near York, he defeated the Scandinavians but then, hearing the Normans had landed on the south coast, he had to march south again.

The battle did not take place at Hasting's, from which it takes it names, but at Senlac, six and three-quarters miles north-west.

Harold decided to take up a defensive position and waited for William to attack. The armies were roughly similar in number, each probably totalling 9,000. Harold had an elite force of 2,000 house-carles, whose principal weapon was the axe. The remainder of his army consisted of the *fyrd*, a kind of territorial army led by thanes but with varying standards of weapon and armour.

The Normans had feudal cavalry which they had transported from France, well-armoured foot soldiers and a contingent of archers.

The battle began at 9am and lasted all day. The Normans charged at the English positions repeatedly but made little impact. Two circumstances helped them to final victory. During the battle groups of Harold's *fyrdsmen* pursued their opponents down the slope but then fell easy prey to charges by the Norman cavalry. A similar manoeuvre was repealed at least twice.

Towards the end of the afternoon, when both sides were very tired, William ordered his archers to aim high into the air to dislodge the English by falling arrows. It was probably at this stage that Harold was killed, possibly by an arrow in the eye just as the Normans were making their final onslaught. The shock of seeing their leader fall caused the English line to crumble and several knights burst through. A group of housecarls fought a desperate rearguard action, but amidst general slaughter. William took possession of the field.

LEWES

Second Barons' War

A Battle Lost by Recklessness

1264

Henry III had succeeded to the throne as a child in 1216, but throughout his 56-year reign never learnt wisdom. By 1258 his liking for foreign favourites and his tendency to ignore the advice of the barons had made his extremely unpopular. The leader of the baronial faction was Simon de Montfort, formerly a close friend of the King, but now a vigorous opponent of Henry's arbitrary policies.

Words turned to blows in April 1264 when both sides moved to secure for themselves the strategic castles throughout the realm. The King's party was successful in the Midland's and south-west, mainly through the dash of Prince Edward, who later became Edward I. However, de Montfort held London.

The main armies eventually met outside, Lewes, Sussex, on 14th May, 1264. Henry's supporters (under John, Earl de Warenne) held the town and castle. De Montfort drew up his army on Cliffton Hill and advanced towards the town. He personally commanded the right wing, de Clare the centre, and de Segrave the left. Henry himself the centre and Prince Edward the right.

De Montfort pressed hard on Henry, who fought well. Prince Edward put in a powerful cavalry charge and swept away the opposing wing, which was largely composed of untrained Londoners, many of whom were drowned in the River Ouse. Prince Edward pursued too far and when he returned found that the main battle had been lost. Some of Henry's knights tried to escape across the river, which is tidal, but stuck in the mud. When the tide receded they were seen, drowned but still in their saddles. Henry III and Prince Edward were taken prisoner. Richard of Cornwall took refuge in a windmill but was discovered and captured. Of the 9,000 on each side some 600 died.

De Montfort had won the battle by his quick grasp of the tactical situation, for when Prince Edward left the field in pursuit it was clear that the battle must be decided before he could return. The rebels therefore concentrated on capturing the King himself with a desperate thrust against the royalist centre.

By the Mise (settlement) of Lewes, de Monffort became master of the Kingsom, but only a year later he was to meet Henry again at Evesham.

EVESHAM

Second Barons' War

The Fall of de Montfort

1265

During the summer of 1265, the downfall of de Montfort, Earl of Leicester and master of England was being planned by his enemies. Prince Edward, King Henry's son, had escaped from Simon's clutches and put his hand to an alliance with Gilbert de Clare, Earl of Gloucester, and the disaffected Roger Mortimer. Both men were Marcher lords, holding great estates and resources of castles and fighting men on the Welsh border.

To meet this threat de Montfort made a treaty with Llewelyn, Prince of Wales, who promised to ravage the lands of the rebellious Marcher lords. Then, during July, de Montfort and a small force campaigned against the Marchers, but he was outmanoeuvred. His enemies managed to cut off all the crossings of the Severn, leading de Montfort dangerously isolated on the west bank. Yet the trap was far from sprung for de Montfort's son, Simon the younger, was approaching from the east with an army.

The elder de Monfort's hope lay with his son, for his own forces, including Welsh footmen, were outnumbered by Prince Edward and the Marchers. Prince Edward recognised this and decided that his best chance was to strike at the younger de Montfort before he joined his father. Fortunately for Edward, young Simon and his troops moved slowly and when they reached Kenilworth castle were unaware of the nearness of their foes. Marching by night, Prince Edward surprised his foes; many, like the Earl of Oxford, were asleep in their beds. Young de Montfort took refuge in the castle and most of his barons and knights were captured.

Unaware of this disaster, the old Earl had crossed the Severn at Worcester and moved to Evesham to await his son and reinforcements. On the morning of 4th August, his men saw the banners of an approaching army which they took to be the expected host of young Simon. Soon, however, the keen-eyed saw Prince Edward's banner and the red chevrons of de Clare. The Earl's forces lay within a loop of the Avon with a bridge as the only means of escape. Drawing his men into a column, he threw himself on the main host of his foes. De Clare's men struck his flank and he and his close allies stood and fought together. Henry de Montfort, his son went down, as did the other lords of his party, and at last the Earl died, fighting bravely in the thick of the melee.

BANNOCKBURN

First War of Scottish Independence

A Famous Scottish Victory

1314

On 24th June 1314 a Scottish army under Robert Bruce decisively defeated an English army commanded by Edward II, at Bannockburn two miles south of Stirling.

For several years Bruce had been engaged in uniting the Scots and retaking castles which had formerly been held by England. In 1313 he captured Edinburgh and Roxburgh and laid siege to Stirling. Edward II was a poor general with a little heart for war, but he felt that the loss of Scottish territories which his father had won might jeopardise his own position if he made no attempt to recover them. Accordingly he raised an army said to have been 100,000 but probably a quarter of that figure. Although well-equipped, it was heavily burdened with siege weapons and unnecessary luxuries.

The Scots, on the contrary, were very lightly equipped and armed. They had a smaller army than the English, but had the advantage of being able to choose and prepare the ground for the battle. Bruce knew that the tidal waters of the Forth contributed to making the marshy ground treacherous and changeable; what might be firm at low tide could be impassable several hours later.

Bruce waited with his army between the marsh and a small mound, Gillies Hill. In front of his position he dug numerous pits, which he filled with sharp stakes and covered over. On the first day of the battle the English cavalry charged continually at that sector but failed to break through. By evening casualties were so high that Edward decided to break off the attack. He camped on ground near the Forth, but during the night his supply train failed to reach him across the marshy ground. At dawn the Scots closed in and caught the English in a cramped position in which they could not manoeuvre. Showers of Scottish arrows completed their discomfiture. Instead of rallying his men and mounting a counter-attack Edward left the battlefield, intent only on his own safety. The English defeat was completed when a horde of Scottish camp-followers, hoping for loot, streamed from the hill towards the battlefield. The English thought they were Scottish reinforcements and fled.

The victory had a great effect on Scottish morale and is often said to be the beginning of the unification of Scotland.

EDWARD II.

THE MEMORIAL CROSS

BATTLE OF BOROUGHBRIDGE

THE DEVIL'S ARROWS
ON THE BATTLEFIELD

BOROUGHBRIDGE

Despenser War

Great Lancaster's Fall

1322

In March 1322, the mighty Earl of Lancaster was a fugitive. With about 700 fighting men including many knights of his own retinue, he was fleeing across Yorkshire. Behind him was the larger army of the wilful and feckless Edward II, determined to destroy the Earl. For the past 12 years Lancaster had been the focus of baronial opposition, vainly trying to control the wayward King. Now he was isolated, his castles had fallen and many of his sworn men and allies had crept away to seek the King's grace and pardon. Edward, propped up by his rapacious favourites the Despensers, was eager for revenge.

At Boroughbridge, Lancaster, his ally the Earl of Hereford, and their small army sought to cross the Ure. Facing him, on the north bank, were the archers and mounted men of the northern shires, raised by Andrew de Harclay, Warden of Carlisle. Lancaster called on Harclay for passage over the bridge. The King, he argued, was in the hands of worthless favourites, and if Harclay gave way, he would gain vast lands.

Bribes were in vain, and on 16th March Lancaster's forces divided in two, one attempted to cross the bridge while the other tried to force a nearby ford. The archers and men-at-arms beat them back. Horses and men went down and the Earl of Hereford was speared as he stood on the bridge, taken unawares by a Welsh pikemen who had crept underneath him. The arrows of Harclay's archers took a grim toll of the rebel forces and they lost stomach for further fight.

Lancaster was forced to beg an armistice until the next morning, but during the night there were numerous desertions and his men scattered, some changing their rich armour for peasants' clothes. The Earl was taken, and brought, amid the cheers of his enemies, to his own great hall at Pontefract. There his peers found him guilty of treason and he was taken out into the snow to be beheaded. Despite attempts to humiliate him, he was dressed in a penitential gown and mounted 'on a lene white Jade with owt Bridil', and executed to the jeers of a hostile crowd, he died bravely. He was buried with little ceremony by the monks of Pontefract near the high altar of their priory church.

Edward II was now unchallenged master of England. But within five years, he, the Despensers and Harclay would have died cruel deaths.

SLUYS

The Hundred Years War

A Most Complete Naval Battle

1340

At the start of the Hundred Years War, before the English could campaign in France, they first had to secure the English Channel. In 1340 Edward III with 147 ships and 3,500 men-at-arms sailed to do battle with a French fleet concentrated at the port of Sluys, in Flanders. Unlike Edward, Philip IV of France had no intention of risking his life in the battle and remained in Paris.Philip IV had, however, engaged the services of a Mediterranean sea rover. A Genoese captain called Barbanera brought a squadron of 27 galleys to strengthen the French. Ignoring the Genoese advice to sail out and fight the English, the French admirals chose to moor their ships in three long lines in the roadsteads of Sluys. The French warships were lashed together and there in a defensive formation they passively awaited the arrival of the English.

Edward made the most of his tactical advantage. After scouts had disembarked and made careful reconnaissance of the French deployments. Edward moved into position on 24th June and awaited the right moment. At noon, with the wind and tide at their most favourable, and the sun at his back, Edward ordered the fleet to attack. Edward's squadrons, to the sound of trumpets and kettledrums, and the cry of St. George' rammed the first of the French lines.

At this time, sea fighting was little more than an extension of land warfare. The main weapon was the boarding party, with fire support from arrow, lime, flame and stone. Edward's tactics were simple and brutally efficient. He was able to mass three of his ships to one of the enemy.

The battle lasted nine hours and men perished in their thousands. Barbanera escaped with his squadrons; otherwise the French fleet was totally destroyed. Admiral Quieret was killed, and Admiral Behuchet was hanged from a yardarm by Edward, as a reprisal for earlier burning Portsmouth.

CRECY

The Hundred Years War

The Supremacy of the Longbow

1346

Crecy was the first great land battle of the Hundred Years War. In part the cause was the rivalry between Philip VI of France and Edward III of England. The French King claimed that the Englishman was his vassal by right of holding a French title in Aquitaine; Edward III countered this by claiming the French throne through his mother's family. War broke out in 1337 after Philip had declared Gascony forfeit but not until July 1346 could Edward muster an adequate expeditionary force. He disembarked 15,000 men near Cherbourg and then marched towards the north east, to link up with the Flemish allies near Bethune.

Although Edward had difficulty in finding a place to cross the Somme, he eventually did so near Abbeville. Philip had brought up a huge army to intercept the English force, and this crossed the Somme soon afterwards. Edward turned to give battle and drew up his army in a well-chosen position on the forward slope of the hill, east of the Crecy-Wadicourt road. His army, now numbering 9000, was divided into three 'battles' (sections), two forward and one in reserve.

The right flank 'battle' was commanded by the Black Prince, the left by the Earl of Northampton, and the rear (reserves) by Edward III himself. The longbowmen were positioned so that they could fire obliquely into the French lines. In front of the English positions, pits were dug to check cavalry charges. The French had Genoese crossbowmen, but these were exhausted by the long march and also had wet bowstrings after a sudden shower of rain. In contrast, the English longbowmen, who could protect their bowstrings, sent volley after volley of arrows into the French knights and horses at a range of some 240 metres. Exasperated by the failure of their own bowmen, the French knights hacked a way through these to reach the English. However, they were overwhelmingly defeated, and the English force marched on to besiege Calais. The King's ally, the blind King of Bohemia, had also rushed into the battle and was killed; along with the flower of French chivalry. The longbow in skilled hands had provided a devastating weapon.

This crushing victory established the importance of the longbow and made England a greatly feared military power. It also enhanced the reputation of the Black Prince. 1500 French knights were killed, but English losses were very small.

NEVILLE'S CROSS

Second War of Scottish Independence

The Scots Overthrown

1346

When Edward III made war on France in 1337, he had feared a Franco-Scottish alliance and invasion from the North. His forebodings were fulfilled in 1345, when the forces of David II of Scotland ravaged the lands around Carlisle. Urged on by the French King, David mounted a second raid into England in 1346, this time into Northumberland and Durham.

Edward, then campaigning in northern France, had anticipated such an attack. He had not drawn troops from north of the Trent, so the northern barons, Henry, Lord Percy and Ralph, Lord Neville were able to call up troops to beat back the invaders. The Scots army made its way south through Northumberland to Durham, burning villages and carrying off sheep, oxen and bullocks. The Scottish marauders were intercepted by the northern levies at Neville's Cross, just outside Durham, on 17th October. Here the Scots formed their traditional formations, schiltroms. These consisted of pikemen in hedgehog-like masses. Lightly armoured, the Scots found themselves helpless under the arrow showers of the northern bowmen. The outcome of the battle was assured and the broken Scots, unable to come to grips with their tormentors, were routed. A Northumberland squire, John Coupland, was able, in the scrimmage after the battle, to capture King David.

The Scots King was conducted to London and imprisoned in the Tower where he stayed until 1356. His ransom was set as 100,000 crowns, and the lucky Coupland was granted an annuity of £500. King David grew to like the English, and his conversion expressed itself in his suggestion of 1364 that the crowns of England and Scotland should be united after his death. Such views found little sympathy from his heir, Robert the Steward, who had controlled Scotland during the King's absence and was later to come to the throne as Robert II, the first of the Stuart kings.

If Edward had hoped that the Scots King, a prisoner in London, was the key to a biddable Scotland, he was mistaken. Thanks to Robert the Steward, the Scots continued to threaten England's northern border, and in 1355 Edward had to tour the area in order to assure himself of its readiness to meet any future invasions.

RADCOT BRIDGE

Richard II Thwarted

1387

Between 1385 and 1387 England drifted towards civil war. The source of the crisis was the behaviour of the young King, Richard II. He was anxious to stamp his own on his Government and introduce new practices.

The nobility were alarmed by Richard's schemes. In 1385 and 1386, Parliament, still the mouthpiece of a small clique of noblemen, attempted to impose restraints on the King. Richard was incensed, especially when in 1386 the "Wonderful" Parliament imposed conditions on his freedom of action. Ranged against him were his uncle, Thomas, Duke of Gloucester, his cousin, Henry Bollingbroke, Earl of Derby and the Earls of Warwick, Nottingham and Arundel.

To meet their combined power, the King sought ways to raise an army. During 1387 he toured England in an attempt to stir up support for his cause. At Shrewsbury, he met with the judges, specially summoned, and got from them a declaration that Parliament could not bind him or limit his Royal rights. Backed by the opinions of the wisest men of the law, the King looked for the means to uphold their claims. In Cheshire, where the Crown owned great estates, he raised an army of men-at-arms and archers, each wearing his badge of the white hart with a golden chain – the 'riche hart' which punned his name. Over confident he returned to London. His enemies guessed his intensions and prepared themselves. The five noblemen called out their retainers and began to concentrate their forces to meet any sudden move to Richard. On 17th November they faced the King and called for the punishment of his favourites.

The King was adamant, His closest favourite, Robert de Vere, Earl of Oxford (created Duke of Ireland by Richard in a typical flurry of fancy) was moving south from Cheshire with a fighting army. The five nobles withdrew west from London with their forces, planning to intercept de Vere as his army crossed the Cotswold. De Vere and his forces, seeking a crossing of the Thames, were caught in the fog at Radcot Bridge, west of Oxford, on 20th December. The King's favourite found the Earl of Derby in front of him at Radcot and the Duke of Gloucester closing in behind him. In a brief skirmish, the Cheshire men were scattered and de Vere escaped. The nobles, triumphant, returned to London to face the King, now powerless.

SHREWSBURY

Glyn Dwr Rising

Won by Good Tactics

1403

When Henry of Bollingbroke deposed his cousin Richard II, and made himself King of England as Henry IV, he was soon to be faced with major problems. First he encountered insurgency by Richard's friends, next a Welsh rebellion led by Owain Glyn Dwr, and then invasion from Scotland. The last of these were defeated by an army led by Henry Percy, Earl of Northumberland. The Percy family were redoubtable warriors who had materially assisted Henry to the throne. In the Battle of Homildon Hill on 14th September they defeated the Scots and took many prisoners.

However, instead of being allowed to accept large ransoms for their prisoners, the Percies were ordered to hand them over to Henry, who was desperately short of money and needed the ransoms.

Disgusted at the treatment, Northumberland planned a rebellion in which he would be assisted by the Scots, the French and the Welsh, His son Harry, known as 'Hotspur', then marched his army to Shrewsbury where he expected to be joined by Glyn Dwr.

Shrewsbury was a vital strategic point as it commanded the passage of the Severn. Henry IV reached it before the rebels because he had marched 41 miles in one day. Glyn Dwr did not appear – delayed by floods he was still in Carmarthen.

Frustrated in his attempt to reach the town first, Hotspur drew up his army on a slope three miles away and waited for Henry to take the initiative. The Royal Army had an advantage in numbers, being 14,000 to 11,000, and both armies had a good supply of archers. After the opening volleys of arrows the armies clashed but Henry, using superb tactics, closed a pincer movement on the weak point in Hotspur line. Prince Henry, the future Henry V, was wounded in the face by an arrow but Hotspur himself, who had been encircled, was killed with a spear.

There was much uncertainty among the rebels. The Scots and English had recently been enemies and did not co-operate easily. Henry IV dressed up several of his retainers to resemble him and this confused the rebels attacks, The death of Hotspur caused the rebels to lose heart and flee. The Earl of Northumberland, who was not at the battle, was fined heavily and stripped of offices and castles for his part in the rebellion.

AGINCOURT

The Hundred Years War

God for Harry

1415

Henry V's major aim on his accession in 1413 was the recapture of the lost territories in France. Accompanied by knights, men-at-arms and archers, Henry set sail for France in August 1415.

The army landed in Normandy, and Henry laid siege to Harfleur, which he did not take until mid-September. With an army weakened by disease and reduced to 6000 Henry's plan to advance on Paris was abandoned. He decided instead to make for his other possession, Calais, further to the north-east, through enemy territory. He marched to the River Somme, which was guarded by French troops, but by moving up-river he managed to find a safe crossing place. However, the large army was now between him and Calais.

The French chose the most favourable battlefield they could find – a large newly-sown cornfield. Half way down the field on one side was Agincourt, surrounded by trees, and on the other the village of Tramecourt.

Henry's army spread out between the two villages, with the French army, possibly numbering 50,000, in front. Henry's men-at-arms were in the centre, and on the wings, by the edge of the woods, were the archers, who placed tall stakes in front of them to break the inevitable cavalry charge.

The French were drawn up in three lines, with mounted troops on each side. As Henry's archers opened fire the French cavalry moved forward to attack them. They could not pass their stakes, and many were cut down by arrows as they moved into the centre of the field.

After initially giving ground, the English line held as the French advanced. As the great host moved forward the press became intolerable and man-oeuvre impossible. The heavily armoured men were easy targets for the archers who, as arrows ran out, moved in with hatchets. Further attempts to advance resulted in more confusion: the French were so tightly wedged they were unable to wield their weapons. In the course of three hours the French army was effectively destroyed. Over 1500 knights and 5000 men-at-arms were killed. English losses were less than 300.

When the slaughter of less valuable prisoners was over, Henry's army moved on to Calais. Agincourt was a great victory for English arms against far superior forces, and it established Henry's reputation. However, in practical terms the campaign gained little.

CASTILLON

The Hundred Years War

The Fall of Gascony

1453

By 1450 Charles VII of France had driven the last English soldier from Normandy. His mind next turned to the Duchy of Gascony, which for 200 years had been under English rule, and whose inhabitants maintained a warm affection for their English overlords. The French occupied Bordeaux while in England, already disintegrating under the inept rule of Henry VI, noble factions jockeyed for power.

Distracted by internal disorder and plagued by aristocratic feuds, the English Government vainly looked for men and money with which to hold the valuable Duchy. In October 1452, John Talbot, Earl of Shrewsbury, the aged veteran of the French wars, landed in Gascony and the people of Bordeaux expelled the French garrison. Not long after, in March 1453 his son, Lord Lisle, landed with 210 men-at-arms and 2,325 archers. In England plans were in hand for further reinforcements of over 2,000 men under William

Lord Say.

Shrewsbury had over 7,000 men under his command in July when the French army advanced once again. Charles VII opened his campaign with a siege of Castillon, 44 kn east of Bordeaux. Earthworks were dug around the town and the King's great guns began to pummel its walls. Shrewsbury marched to save the town and on 17th July attacked the French siege works. Under cannon fire and facing a spirited resistance, the English were beaten back.

Nevertheless, the outcome of the battle remained in doubt until the unexpected entry into the conflict of a force of Bretons, who had so far remained concealed in nearby woods. This onslaught of hand-picked soldiers, together with the French superiority in artillery, forced the English to flee in some disorder to the banks of the River Dordogne. Here the old Earl had his famous white palfrey shot from under him. Pinned and defenceless under his mount, Talbot was killed by a battle-axe blow to the skull. His corpse was discovered the next day so badly disfigured that it was only identified by a missing tooth. The English forces finally broke and withdrew to Bordeaux. In England, a shortage of cash prevented the relief force from sailing; Bordeaux was taken and English dominion in France was ended. Shrewsbury name lived on, for the French remembered the campaign as the war of 'Roi Talabot', a token of the reputation of a formidable soldier.

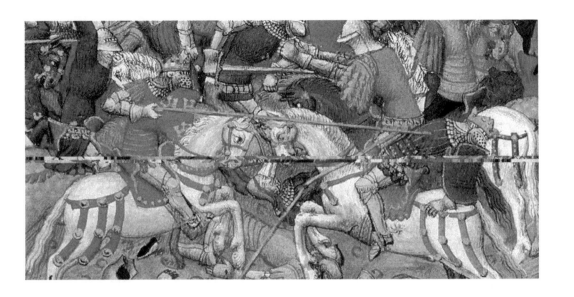

TOWTON

Wars of the Roses

The Struggle for the Crown

1461

In March 1461 there were two kings in England. In York, Henry VI held state, the rightful heir of Lancaster, upheld by the forces of the northern nobility. In London, Edward IV, the 19 year old son of Richard, Duke of York, was proclaimed rightful king. From all over southern and eastern England, fighting men came to him, determined to uphold his cause. The clash of arms between the two armies would decide who sat on the throne and ruled England.

It was a time of violence and uncertainty. In the South men feared the rapacity of the northerners who had, in the past month, ravaged the countryside through which they had passed on their abortive march to London. From the cities and towns of southern England men therefore rallied to the Yorkists. The men of Worcester marched under the banner of a wolf, those from Northampton under a "wildcat" and the forces from Leicester beneath a 'griffin'. No doubt they would have swelled the Yorkist host as it moved slowly along the Great North Road.

By 28th March, King Edward and his forces had concentrated at Ferry-bridge. There were upwards of 15,000 men under his orders, sufficient to challenge the rather large numbers of Lancastrians drawn up in a sprawling line a few miles to the north. The day of the battle, 29th March, was Palm Sunday and a bitter wind blew on the backs of the Yorkists and carried slurries of snow into their enemies' faces. The Yorkists vanguard of archers under the command of Lord Fauconberg opened the fight with a shower of arrows. These fell upon the Lancastrians who replied, but to no avail for the wind made their arrows fall short. Fauconberg ordered his bowmen to pick up their opponents' arrows and return them.

The fight lasted for six or seven hours with a huge melee of men-at-arms hacking and lunging across the ridge where the Lancastrians had taken their position. No advantage was gained until the Duke of Norfolk re-inforced the Yorkist right. Slowly, the Lancastrian line was turned and the fugitives were crowded Cock Beck, which bordered the Lancastrian right. Hundreds drowned as the fight became a rout. No mercy was asked for or given. The Lord Dacre and the Earl of Northumberland was killed. King Henry and his lords turned and fled north; for the moment, Edward IV was unchallenged King of England.

BARNET

Wars of the Roses

The Fight in the Fog

1471

On 13th April 1471, Edward IV, with an army of perhaps 6,000 men, marched north out of London to find and bring to battle the forces of the Earl of Warwick. Warwick, once Edward's chief prop, was marching south with an army of similar size comprising his own retainers and those of his Lancastrian allies. In the evening, some of Edward's scouts entered Barnet where they discovered and routed a party of Warwick's advance-guard. The Royal army moved through the town and pitched camp a mile or so to the north. By this time it was dark and a few hundred yards off were the tents of Warwick's troops. The Earl 'thinking greatly to annoy the King's host' fired his guns through the night, but the King ordered his men to be still and wait for the dawn.

Just after four the next morning, the King roused his troops and ordered them to their battle stations. A thick early morning midst covered the ground between the armies and men could see for only a few yards.

Edward placed his men in three masses, known as 'battles', that on the right under his younger brother, Richard, Duke of Gloucester, the centre under his own command, and the left under William, Lord Hastings. So ordered, the Royal army moved into the gloom and towards their enemies. Inside Warwick's army there was unease, for many suspected the shifting conscience of the Earl and feared he might defect. He was advised to fight on foot, for mounted he could easily flee. His right flank was under the Earl of Oxford, his left under the Duke of Essex, whilst he took command in the centre.

The two armies plodded through the mist and collided. In the murk light, it was soon apparent to Oxford that he had unintentionally outflanked Hasting's men who, surprised, were quickly routed. The Lancastrians pursued and reached Barnet which they looted. Oxford rallied some men and rushed back through the fog, hoping to hit the Yorkists in the rear. He lost his way and blundered into a party of Warwick's men. They saw his men wearing the white star of de Vere, thought it was the Yorkist rising sun badge, and attacked. Oxford, thinking himself betrayed, fled crying "Treason". The cry was taken up and the hard-pressed Lancastrians scattered. Warwick was slain 'somewhat fleeing' and the rest of his forces were forced back in flight by Edward, who had shown much courage during the fight.

TEWKESBURY

Wars of the Roses

The Eclipse of Lancaster

1471

On 16th April 1471, Queen Margaret, her son, Edward, and a handful of Lancastrian lords landed in Weymouth. They were greeted by baleful news. Her husband, Henry VI, was a prisoner of Edward IV her ally Warwick, the kingmaker, lay at the battle of Barnet.

Undismayed, the Queen made her plans. Backed by the Duke of Somerset and the Earl of Devon, she moved through the south-western shires and raised men. Local feeling was for Lancaster and by the time she reached Bristol, her efforts and those of the local nobility had created an army of over 3,000. The Lancastrian objective was Gloucester, where the army could bridge the Severn and link up with Jasper Tudor, Earl of Pembroke, who was raising men in western Wales. Her forces moved northwards through the Vale of Berkeley but on reaching Gloucester found their way barred by its governor, Sir Richard Beauchamp, a knight loyal to Edward IV.

A few miles behind the frustrated Lancastrians, high on the Cotswold ridge, was the army of Edward IV. The King had moved swiftly, thanks to the reports of his spies. From London he moved into Gloucestershire, and his forces followed the Queen's army as, tired, it dragged itself to Tewkesbury.

Here, on 4th May, the Lancastrians, weary and tired of pursuit, turned at bay. The Lancastrians, their backs to the small town, faced their foes over a countryside of 'evil lanes and deep dykes, so many hedges, trees and bushes'. Each army was split into three battalions and the Yorkists opened with a bombardment of guns which 'sore oppressed' their enemies. The young Duke of Somerset, making use of a sunken lane, attempted to outflank the Yorkists. His stratagem failed for Edward had posted 200 or so spearmen as a caution against such a ploy. Somerset suspected a trick and in his rage struck down his fellow commander, Lord Wenlock. Whilst their leaders killed each other, the Lancastrians were forced back and routed. There died Margaret's son, Prince Edward, and the next day Somerset and many others were wrenched from sanctuary in the abbey and executed. Margaret was taken prisoner, orders were given for the murder of Henry IV, and Edward was at last without enemies in England.

BOSWORTH

Wars of the Roses

The Beginning of Modern Britain

1485

The Battle of Bosworth on 22nd August 1485 marked the end of the medieval period of history and the long conflict between the Yorkists and the Lancastrians. Richard III, a Yorkist, had been King of England for two years. He was already suspected of evil deeds and was feared to be a tyrant. Henry Tudor, a Lancastrian in exile, collected 2000 supporters and landed in Wales in August 1485. More joined him and as he approached the Midlands, his army numbered 5,000.

Richard had positioned himself at Nottingham with 10,000 and, hearing of Henry's approach, moved to Bosworth and set out his army on the long ridge between Sutton Cheney and Shenton. Each army had some cannon and a few handgunners but relied mainly on archers and infantry. The ground over which Henry's army advanced was wet and marshy, and as he was an inexperienced general, the outlook for the Lancastrians seemed poor.

However, Richard had enemies among his own supporters and the Earl of Northumberland, with 3,500 infantry, stayed outside the battle.

Richard's principal aide, the Duke of Norfolk, fought with skill in the centre and forced the Lancastrians back. At this point Lord Stanley, with 2,500, changed sides and attacked the King's men. Richard attempted to reach and kill Henry but his horse stumbled in the marsh, spilling its rider. Richard is reputed to have shouted 'A horse my kingdom for a horse' but was quickly surrounded by the Lancastrians and killed. His body was stripped and displayed naked. The treacherous Stanley picked up the crown and put it on Henry's head. Norfolk was killed in the battle. Northumberland never engaged. There was no massacre after the battle and only three people were executed. Later Henry married Elizabeth of York. With the birth of their son, Henry VIII, the Tudor dynasty was established.

Bosworth, although one of the most important battles of English history, was small in numbers. It was a victory for treachery not skill. Richard, whatever his faults was a brave and experienced soldier. Betrayal by his subordinates rather than the skills of his opponents caused his defeat in battle and his downfall.

STOKE

Wars of the Roses

Yorkist Challenge to Henry VII

1487

In 1485 at the Battle of Bosworth, Henry VII, representing the Lancastrians, had won the throne after the long dynastic struggle known as the Wars of the Roses. The Yorkists, however, had not relinquished hope of regaining the throne, and their intrigues centred round Margaret of York who was dowager Duchess of Burgundy, Francis. Viscount Lovell, one of Richard III's closest friends, joined her there with other Yorkist sympathisers. An imposter, Lambert Simnel, was pretending to be Edward, Earl of Warwick, the Yorkist claimant to the throne, and they decided to use him to arouse support. John de la Poole, Earl of Lincoln, another Yorkist champion, joined Simnel in Ireland and the imposter was accepted and crowned as Edward VI in Dublin. Ireland had always favoured the Yorkists and the most powerful noble, the Earl of Kildare, was never unwilling to challenge English power.

Margaret sent an army of 2,000 German mercenaries led by a famous soldier, Martin Schwarz. They raised more troops in Ireland and then crossed to England. Here the rebels were disappointed for they hoped to gain support from old Yorkist families, but failed to do so, even in Lancashire and Yorkshire. England was tired of war and would not be aroused. The King moved towards the rebels with about 5,000 men, backed up by Stanley with 6,000 further soldiers, and the armies clashed south of Newark. Fighting was heavy and it has been estimated that the rebel casualties numbered 4,000. The leaders, including Lincoln, were killed or put to flight, and Lambert Simnel was put to work in the royal kitchen.

Henry immediately offered thanks-giving for his victory, but was concerned to prevent any further Yorkist threats. He initiated an enquiry into those responsible for the uprising and those who had spread false rumours about its success, while parliament passed an Act of Attainder against 28 of the rebels. He persuaded the Pope to excommunicate those Irish bishops who had participated in Lambert Simnel's coronation, but the Irish chiefs were pardoned after taking oaths of allegiance to him. Kildare was allowed to remain Lord Deputy., but was reminded by Henry, 'My masters of Ireland, you will crown apes at last.'

FLODDEN FIELD

War of the League of Cambrai

Bannockburn Revenged

1513

Honouring his French alliance, James IV crossed the Tweed with the great-est ever Scots army, in August, while Henry VIII was campaigning in France. A popular and successful King, he resented Henry's high-handed attitude towards Scotland.

After taking several border castles, James camped on Flodden Hill. The Earl of Surrey mustered an English army at Newcastle and marched north. James named 9th September when Surrey challenged him, but ignored the request for battle on 'a fair field'. The English dared not attack, as a marsh and the River Till protected the Scottish position. At 5 am half the English marched north along the River Till towards a bridge, whilst the rest forded it and were guided across a great bog. They aimed to meet at Branxton Bill, immediately north of Flodden. This daring manoeuvre took six hours. His captains urged action, but James refused to move until the last moment.

Once Surrey's objective became obvious, James hurried to reach Branxton Hill first. His original advantage was lost.

The 30,000 Scots were divided into five bristling masses of pikemen. Their 5½m spears made them deadly advancing over level ground, but the formation was vulnerable from the rear and changed direction with difficulty. James rashly dismounted to fight with his central division. The battle winning weapons of the 25,000 English were the longbow and the halberd, a 2½m combination spear and axe.

In driving rain battle began at 4 pm, but James's cannon failed to find their range and Surrey's could not fire uphill. The Borderers smashed the English right, but then scattered for plunder. When the English withstood the next division, James impetuously charged against Surrey's centre. Meanwhile the English archers routed the Scottish right and swung round to take James in the rear. They bore down just as Surrey's men were giving ground. James fought on defiantly in the dusk until he was slashed down.

10,000 Scots lay dead, and 2,000 English. James's body was eventually recognised in the carnage, surrounded by most of his nobles. Scotland crowned his infant son and awaited invasion. But Surrey wisely made peace, leaving the remaining Scottish lords to squabble for power.

SOLWAY MOSS

Anglo-Scottish Wars

Ignominious Defeat for the Scots

1542

Henry VIII had long cherished hopes of conquering Scotland, and he feared the alliance of France and Scotland against England. In 1540 he sent Sir Ralph Sadler to James V in an unsuccessful attempt to wean the Scottish King from the influence of the powerful Archbishop Beaton, who was the champion of Catholic and French interests in Scotland. In the following year James V promised to meet Henry at York but failed to appear. In the summer of 1542, therefore, Henry ordered the Duke of Norfolk to raise forces in the northern counties for an invasion of Scotland.

James had raised an army to meet the English attack, but the war was unpopular and it disbanded immediately. He was not on good terms with the Scottish nobles as they felt excluded from his councils and resented his favourites. They claimed the war was in the French interest for which they had no desire to fight. James was incensed by the refusal of the nobles to support him, and he raised another army backed by the churchmen. It numbered 10,000 but had no commander initially, and marched towards the border with no overall direction.

On reaching the border Sir Oliver Sinclair, a favourite of the King, announced that he had been appointed to lead the attack, but his command was resented and total disorder ensued. The English army led by Sir Thomas Wharton numbered not more than 3000 men, but it advanced boldly, and waited for the Scots to arrive. The English horsemen were released unexpectedly and the Scots were forced into the marshland of Solway Moss where many drowned. It was an ignominious defeat for Scotland with 1100 prisoners taken, and when the news was conveyed to James V he died of grief, leaving an infant daughter. Mary.

The prisoners captured at Solway Moss were initially imprisoned, but then returned to Scotland to form the nucleus of an English party there. The Scottish Council overthrew Beaton and put the Earl of Arran in power. Henry then forced Scotland to sign the Treaty of Greenwich by which James' daughter Mary was to marry Edward, Prince of Wales. This was a counter-productive move for it revived a national sentiment amongst the Scots. Beaton escaped from prison and re-established his pro=French Catholic policies. Winning the Battle of Solway Moss had not secured Henry's political ambitions in Scotland.

THE SPANISH ARMADA

Anglo-Spanish Wars

The First Modern Sea Battle

1588

The quarrel between England and Spain had been growing since the beginning of Elizabeth's reign (1558), but it was not until 1586 that King Philip decided on the conquest of England.

English ships had been trying to force themselves into the rich trade with the Americas, which Philip wanted to keep as a Spanish monopoly. In the Netherlands English help was prolonging the Dutch revolt despite the efforts of Philip's most able general, the Duke of Parma, and the best army in Europe. Throughout Europe the clash between Reformation and Counter-Reformation was reaching a peak, with England and Spain leading the two sides.

The Spanish Preparation

Spain's first invasion plan involved 90,000 troops and over 500 ships sailing from Spain. However, it was beyond the resources of even the Spanish Empire to raise and supply such a force.

A more modest plan was substituted, with a smaller fleet sailing from Spain to escort the Duke of Parma's army across the Channel. However, in April 1587 Drake raided Cadiz. Here he not only 'singed the King of Spain's beard' but destroyed most of the Armada's supplies. The invasion was therefore postponed for a year. The Armada's original commander died and was replaced by the Marquis of Medina Sidonia. Sidonia had no military experience, but did have the social position to overawe his more expert subordinates. In England preparations for the invasion were also beginning. Troops were raised and forts repaired, but clearly the navy would be the first line of defence.

The Balance of Forces

The opposing fleets were broadly similar in composition. The core of each was about 40 royal ships, the only true warships available. The Spanish ships were generally larger and clumsier than the English, but they carried more heavy guns. The English warships were of a new design, smaller, but much more manoeuvrable than traditional sailing ships and mostly armed with long-ranging guns. On both side the majority were converted merchant ships. In the Spanish fleet these were mostly used as transports, but the English ships were designed to trade or fight. They were therefore similar in design to the Queen's ships, but generally smaller and more lightly armed. In numbers the English had the advantage, 197 ships to the Armada's 130. Against this the Spaniards had more men, 30,000 to 15,000, but too many of these were soldiers. There were more seamen and more trained naval gunners in the English fleet. In leadership the advantage was also with the English fleet. The Spaniards had some experienced commanders, but no one with the personal reputation of a Drake, Hawkins or Frobisher. On both sides there were personal quarrels, but the English were more successful in overcoming these.

The Sailing of The Armada

The Armada sailed from the Tagus on 4th May, but immediately ran into storms and was forced into Coruna. A new start was made on 12th July and three days later the Armada was in the mouth of the Channel. High winds scattered it again, but by 19th July it was reassembled in sight of the Lizard. The Spanish plan was simplicity itself. The Armada would seize a suitable landing place, perhaps Spithead or the Thames, and escort Parma's troops across. A battle with the English fleet was not essential. In outline the English could guess this plan and prepare accordingly. Drake persuaded Lord Howard of Effingham, the fleet's commander, to concentrate at Plymouth. With prevailing westerly winds, Drake wanted to be sure that the English had the advantage of the windward position, and therefore the opportunity to manoeuvre freely. Drake would have preferred to look for the enemy on the Spanish coast, but the fleet was driven back by a storm and forced into Plymouth. It was still there when the Armada appeared. According to tradition, when the news of the Armada's arrival reached Plymouth, Drake and other commanders were playing bowls on Plymouth Hoe. Drake is supposed to have insisted that there was time to finish the game before beating the Dons. This was not just bravado; at the time both wind and tide were driving up Plymouth Sound and no ship of the time could have put to sea against them. Some of the Spanish officers tried to persuade Sidonia to attack the English while they were trapped in port, but he refused, claiming that his orders did not mention Plymouth. Thus he lost his only chance of beating his enemies, for when the English fleet did get to sea, on 20th July, it was able to work to the west and seize the advantage of the windward position. It could now dictate when and how the battle should be fought.

Encounter in the Channel

In this phase of the campaign the Armada moved slowly eastwards along the English coast. Its formation resembled an arrowhead or new moon. Leading in the centre was Medina Sidonia with the most powerful ships. Behind these were the transports, with a squadron mostly of converted merchantmen extending rearwards on either flank. The formation was tightly maintained, but the disadvantage was that the English were now in the Spanish rear, where the weakest ships were. The weather remained fine and for a week the Armada drifted east pursued by the English fleet. There were two main battles, off Plymouth on 21st July and off the Isle of Wight on the 25th. The English exploited the mobility of their ships and the range of their guns, harassing the Spaniards at ranges which their guns could not reach. A few Spanish ships were separated from the main formation and captured, but most were still in good condition when the Armada anchored off Calais on the 27th. Both sides were short of ammunition but only the English could get new supplies.

The fatal flaw in the Spanish plan now appeared. Parma had gathered flat-bottomed boats to transport his troops across the shallows of the Dutch coast and to England. However, they could not defend themselves and the Dutch had a squadron of small ships outside the Spanish ports. The Armada's ships were too big to cross the shallows and get to grips with the Dutch, so it was impossible to join the two halves of the invasion force. Furthermore, while the Armada waited at Calais it was still in reach of the English fleet.

Fireships Wreak Havoc

At midnight on the 28th the English sent fireships drifting down on the Armada. Taken by surprise the Spaniards cut their cables and fled to sea. Morning found them scattered off Gravelines. Having lost their defensive formation they were open to the English attacks, which concentrated on isolated victims. 'We pluck their feathers by little and little,' said Lord Howard. The battle lasted for two days and as the Spanish ships ran out of ammunition the English closed to battering range. The wind grew stronger and began to drive the Spaniards towards the Dutch sandbanks. Many ships had lost their anchors and their masts and rigging were damaged. Just when it seemed that the Armada would be wrecked on the banks the wind changed and allowed it to escape into the North Sea. But hopes of invading England were over.

The Long Run for Home

The only thought was to return to Spain and the only route was northwards around Scotland. The English fleet had now ran out of ammunition itself, but it followed the Armada until 2nd August. Then with provisions running low, and sickness growing, the fleet returned, leaving the Armada to face a series of storms off the west of Scotland and Ireland. In their shattered state the Spanish ships stood little chance. Only 53 of the 130 returned to Spain, most of the rest being wrecked on the Irish coast. Most of the survivors who reached the shore were slaughtered on the spot.

The defeat of the Spanish Armada was a turning point in English and European history. It meant that England would remain Protestant and that the European Protestant would also survive. It checked the growth of Spanish power. For the first time England had influenced history by using seapower, thus setting a pattern for the next three hundred years. The Armada campaign saw the first battles between fleets of gun-armed sailing ships. It is therefore right that 'Armada' is the earliest honour borne by ships of the

Royal Navy.

EDGEHILL

First English Civil War

Opening Clash of the Civil War

1642

When war broke out between King Charles I and Parliament in 1642, the King controlled Wales and the West Country, whilst Parliament held the south-east and east, including London. The midlands and the north were disputed zones. By mid-October Charles' army had grown significantly, and the King decided to take the field and advance on London without delay.

The Royalist force set out from Shrewsbury on the 12th October 1642 and out-manoeuvred a Parliamentary army under the Earl of Essex. Instead of keeping his army between the King and London, Essex let Charles slip past. The problem for the King was whether he should continue on his march to shake Essex off first. Charles decided on the latter course, and on the morning of the 23rd October orders were sent out to occupy the high ridge of Edgehill five miles south-east of Kineton.

Edgehill is a continuous ridge rising 90 metres out of the plain, three miles long facing north-west. The Royalist army numbering some 13,000 men occupied the line of the ridge and the forward slope, and was soon faced by Essex's army of about the same number.

The battle opened with a rather feeble artillery duel. Then Prince Rupert led the Cavalier cavalry in a massed charge against the cavalry of Essex. The Parliamentarians, overwhelmed by the sight of such a formidable force, fled the field of battle. Rupert's cavalry swept on in pursuit and reached the town of Kineton. The Cavalier pursuit effectively robbed the King of his cavalry for an important part of the battle. A combined Roundhead attack by infantry and uncommitted cavalry on the King's left flank caused the Royalist infantry to retreat in confusion. But Prince Rupert's cavalry returned just in time to prevent a Royalist rout, and both sides then withdrew leaving some 5,000 dead upon the field.

Charles missed the golden opportunity presented by this drawn battle. Although he occupied Banbury and Oxford, the route to London was open. However, by the tme the King resumed the march on his one time capital, the opportunity was lost. Essex had fallen back on the city. Confronted by numerically superior force, the King turned back and both sides occupied their winter quarters.

CROPREDY BRIDGE

First English Civil War

Royalist Hopes Kept Alive

1644

Early in the summer of 1644, Parliamentarian armies under the Earl of Essex and Sir William Waller threatened the King's main base at Oxford. Charles and his army broke out of the city on 3rd June, and the Parliamentarian commanders, having failed to catch him, decided to split up; Essex marched off to the West, and Waller continued to pursue the King.

The morning of 29th June saw both armies marching north from Banbury, on parallel courses, with the River Cherwell between them. Waller, who habitually made good use of the ground, halted on Bourton Hill, three miles north of the townm and observed his enemy. He noted that the Royalists were marching well spread out and, moreover, he enjoyed a slight numerical advantage – over 9,000 men to the King's 8,500.

The Royalist advanced guard speeded up just east of the village of Cropredy: this passed unnoticed at the tail of the Royalist column, and Waller at once decided to exploit the over-extension of the King's army.

He dispatched Lieutenant-General John Middleton against Cropredy Bridge to cut through part of the Royalist column, while he himself crossed the Cherwell at Slat Mill ford to attack the Royalist rearguard.

Good though Waller's plan was, it speedily came to grief. Middleton initially made good progress, but he was soon briskly attacked by the King's Lifeguard under Lord Bernard Stuart and by cavalry under Cleveland and Wilmot. Middleton's men were forced back over Cropredy Bridge, and 14 Parliamentarian guns, deployed just east of the bridge, fell into Royalist hands.

Waller was also in difficulties. The Earl of Northampton, commanding one of the brigades of the rearguard, vigorously counter-attacked and drove Waller's men back across the ford.

Waller then fell back into Bourton Hill, leaving small detachments to hold Cropredy Bridge and the ford at Slat Hill. The Royalists attacked both these forces, and made some progress at Slat Hill but little at the bridge. The fighting then died away and, although both armies remained in the field all night, the Royalists, having heard that enemy reinforcements were on the way, marched off in good order the next day.

It was a cheap victory for Charles. Waller lost 700 men, and there were few Royalist casualties.

MARSTON MOOR

First English Civil War

Parliament Gains the North

1644

'I command and conjure you, by the duty and affection which I know you bear me, and all new enterprises laid aside, you immediately march... with all your force to the relief of York.' King Charles I wrote this order to his nephew, Prince Rupert, on 14th June 1644. The Prince accordingly marched upon the city and raised the siege. On 2nd July he set out to meet his enemies on Marston Moor.

The northern Parliamentarian forces and their Scots allies gathered just south of the Long Martson-Tockwith road, on rising ground. Between them, they mustered approximately 28,000 men. The Royalist position lay due north, on the low, flat ground on the other side of the road, with a 'wide and deep' ditch, running parallel with the road, forming the front of their position.

Rupert's men had been waiting on the battlefield since early morning, but the bulk of the Marquis of Newcastle's forces did not appear until mid-afternoon, swelling Rupert's army to rather more than 17,000 men. It was agreed to attack next day, and Newcastle retired to his coach for a quiet pipe of tobacco. The Royalists were thus caught unprepared when the Allied army, horse, foot and dragoons, suddenly advanced at a 'running march'.

Rain swept the battlefield, extinguishing the musket-matches of Rupert's forlorn hope lining the ditch. The Roundheads were soon through to the Royalist main body, where fierce fighting ensued. Some soldiers on both sides fled in panic – a 'shoal of Scots' were seen, crying 'Wae's us, we are all undone', and Rupert had to rally his own men, shouting 'Swounds, do you run, follow me'. The Royalist horse fought hard, but was overcome by Roundheads, and Rupert was obliged to hide in a bean field.

The last phase of the battle began with the Royalist foot almost intact, but now they were exposed to the onslaught of Cromwell's horse. Newcastle's Whitecoats and a brigade of Greencoats made a valiant stand, and it was ony after their ammunition was expended that they succumbed: 'every man fell in the same order and rank wherein he had fought'. Thus passed the immortal Whitecoats and as the last hedge of pikes collapsed beneath the harvest moon, so died the last hopes of Rupert's army. By 9 pm the battle was over, and all hope of Royalist victory in the North was lost.

NASEBY

First English Civil War

Decisive Battle of the Civil War

1645

After the Royalist sack of Leicester, Sir Thomas Fairfax determined to force a decisive action upon Charles I and Prince Rupert. Abandoning the blockade of Oxford, the New Model Army surprised some Cavaliers at Naseby on 13th, and the King was advised to fight, despite his numerical disadvantage.

On the 14th the Royalist army, 9,000 men and 12 guns, drew up along Dust Hill facing Naseby. In the centre Lord Ashley commanded 3,000 foot and the guns; on his left, Sir Marmaduke Langdale drew up 1,500 cavalry; on Astley's right Prince Maurice, Rupert's brother, paraded 1,800 more. The King remained in the rear with the reserve. North of Naseby Fairfax deployed his 13,000 men and 13 cannons. Skippon with 6,000 foot faced Astley; on the right, Oliver Cromwell, second in command, led 3,000 horsemen; on the left General Ireton commanded as many more. Colonel

Okey's dragoons occupied Sulby Hedges on the extreme left, extending towards Maurice's horsemen, whilst Colonel Pride led the small reserve.

The Royalists advanced to attack, Rupert taking command of the right wing. After waiting for Astley's foot to come up, Rupert charged Ireton with fair success, whilst Astley drove into the first line of Roundhead infantry and Skippon was seriously wounded. As Ireton strove to aid his discomfited troops, Rupert's second line attacked his flank and drove the Parliamentary left from the field, Rupert pursued them as far the wagon-laager near Naseby, but was repulsed by its guard.

Meanwhile on the other flank Cromwell forced back Langdale, and fell up on Astley's flank. So far the fortunes of war were pretty even, and had the King now sent in reseve of 930 horse and 700 foot the day might have been won. But the Earl of Carnwath dissuaded him, and a mistaken order sent his Lifeguard off in the wrong direction.

Although Rupert at last rejoined the King, the chance of victory had passed. Colonel Okey remounted his dragoons and charged the isolated Astley's right flank. Beset on three sides., the Royalist infantry began to surrender. The King and his horsemen rode off for Leicester, hotly pursued.

The Royalists had lost 4,000 men; the New Model Army about 1,000. The King's luggage train was captured, including his treasure and his papers, which revealed damaging intrigues with the Irish and foreign powers; the King had effectively lost the war.

WORCESTER

English Civil War

The Rout of the Royalist

1651

The Battle of Worcester was one of the most important battles of the English Civil War, and marked the climax of Oliver Cromwell's military career. It was a hard fought battle for, although the Royalists were outnumbered, they did not admit defeat easily. Cromwell described the battle scene saying, "It was as stiff a contest as ever I have seen'. Worcester safeguarded the new English Republic and it was Oliver's last battle.

In 1650 Cromwell returned from Ireland to take command against the Scots, who had proclaimed Charles II King. He defeated them at Dunbar, but could not follow up this victory because of the skill of Leslie, the Scottish general.

Finally, he allowed the Scots, accompanied by Charles, an open road to England. Although Charles marched through traditionally Royalist areas, the expected support did not come. On 22nd August 1651, dejected and exhausted, the King's army, possibly 16,000 strong, came to rest at Worcester.

When Cromwell approached Worcester he had more than 30,000 soldiers. With this superiority he could afford to divide his army. Fleetwood and Lambert to the south and west of Worcester blocked the retreat into Wales. Cromwell to the east blocked the road to London. Worcester was surrounded. On 29th August his artillery on Red Hill opened fire. Then, for the next four days, Cromwell waited. To carry out his plan he needed to collect enough boats to build two bridges.

On 3rd September all was ready. Fleetwood had placed a bridge of boats across the rivers Severn and Teame which allowed his and Cromwell's armies to join forces and advance on Worcester, drawing the net still more tightly. The Royalists came out of the city to prevent this but were pushed back by sheer weight of numbers. Completely hemmed in, Charles led a desperate sally against the troops on Red Hill. The troops there held out long enough to allow Cromwell to cross back over the Severn by the bridge of boats and came to their rescue. When the Royalists' ammunition ran out they used their guns as clubs. Bitter and confused street fighting continued into the night. Over 2000 Charles' soldiers were killed in the battle. Charles and 4000 others escaped; the rest were captured. In a series of dramatic adventures Charles eventually escaped to France.

MEDWAY

Second Anglo-Dutch Wars

Defeat through Complacency

1667

The Battle of the Medway in June 1667 was the final battle in a disastrous Anglo-Dutch war which had begun in 1665. In the first battle, in 1665, Charles II's brother, Duke of York (later to be king as James II) won a fierce battle off Lowestoft. He sunk 16 Dutch ships for the loss of his own and inflicted 5000 casualties, but he did not follow up his victory. The following year Charles put the fleet under the command of two cavalry generals, Monck and Prince Rupert. They were completely out-manoeuvred by the Dutch Admiral, De Ruyter in the murderous four days battle in the Downs in June. In 1666 the Great Plague still raged, but neither this nor the Great Fire, stopped the war. Parliament granted substantial sums of money to Charles to rebuild the navy and make good the losses sustained in the earlier battles. Charles, however, misused the money, and wasted large sums on extravagant building projects. This meant that the fleet was in poor repair and in no condition to fight.

The greatest and most humiliating disaster came when in 1667 a Dutch fleet slipped up the Medway, burnt Chatham Dockyard and destroyed 16 ships. De Ruyter had already burnt an unfinished fort at Sheerness.

Monck, now the Duke of Albemarle, was in charge of the defences at Chatham and tried to block the channel with a chain stretched between Hoo Ness and Gillingham. However, the chain either broke or was unfastened for it failed to stop the Dutch. Albemarle hastily positioned the guns and established an eight-gun battery at Upnor Castle. When the Dutch returned to the attack on the following day with the intention of completing the devastation, the fire from the Upnor battery which included brisk musketry volleys checked the invaders and limited the damage they were able to do. Nevertheless the Dutch fire-ships had destroyed half the Fleet, and the flagship *Royal Charles* was towed away as a prize. The Dutch retired and put to sea.

Fortunately, peace negotiations were already in hand and the war was concluded with the Treaty of Breda. By this Britain was allowed to retain the Dutch colony of New Netherlands. A town there was renamed New York after the King's brother. As a result of the war, there was considerable rebuilding of England's coastal defences, especially along the Thames and Medway, also at Portsmouth, Plymouth and Tynemouth.

SEDGEMOOR

Monmouth Rebellion

Climax of Monmouth's Rebellion

1685

When Monmouth landed at Lyme-Regis from Holland on 11th June, he assembled a force of some 1,000 musketeers and 500 pikemen. Lord Grey was put in command of the then non-existent cavalry, and four small field guns represented artillery.

After gathering about 150 horse, the rebel army was ready to march. At Bridgport the Dorsetshire and Somerset Militia skirmished with the rebels, who then headed north. Meanwhile the regular army made slow progress west, the dragoons reaching Bridgport with blown horses on the 17th, while the infantry plodded steadily along the Bath road.

At Taunton, Monmouth's army swelled to some 6,000 strong, including 1,000 cavalry. Against him Lord Feversham was placed in command of the arriving regulars, and at each turn Monmouth fund his line of advance – on Bristol, Bath, or northwards towards Cheshire – blocked.

He turned south and repelled a royal attack at Phillip's Norton, but had become increasingly despondent about the non-arrival of promised support. Hearing that reinforcements now awaited him in the Somerset marshes, Monmouth moved west to Bridgewater.

Near the village of Westonzoyland on the marshes of Sedgemoor, Monmouth with some 5,000 ill-assorted troops watched Feversham organise his army of 3,000 and resolved to attack the camp that night, 6th July. However, instead of a straightforward frontal attack with the bayonet, he chose an indirect route. This involved crossing several rhines or drainage ditches. In the confusion of crossing the last-but-one, a pistol shot was fired.

Within minutes the royal drummers were beating the alarm. Lord Grey, balked at the Bussex Rhine, a black band of water of unknown depth, turned right along it to seek a crossing. His cavalry came up against the First Guards, who scattered them with well-ordered musket volleys. Monmouth now brought up a regiment of infantry, but nothing could make them plunge across the Bussex Rhine.

Feversham now ordered his reserve cavalry to form up facing the rebels flanks. In the pre-dawn light, his guns having shattered holes in the rebel ranks, Feversham sent in the infantry from the front and the cavalry, on either flank. The rebels broke, and Monmouth fled the field.

BEACHY HEAD

War of the League of Augsburg/Nine Years War

French Channel Victory

1690

As the Nine Years War entered its second year, the French fleet dominated the Channel. Admiral Comte de Tourville commanded 77 ships and could choose his point of attack, whereas the Anglo-Dutch fleet was largely occupied covering William III's new campaign in Ireland, which left only part to contest French superiority in the Channel.

When Tourville appeared in strength off the Lizard and the Cornish coast, the Council of Regency in London ordered Admiral Herbert, Earl of Torrington, to seek battle, despite his numerical inferiority. In late June he was commanding only 56 vessels off the Isle of Wight, and despite misgivings, he sailed west to find the French. The Anglo-Dutch fleet made contact on 30th June, and manoeuvred to place their ships to windward of the French, forming a line of battle. The van comprised five Dutch vessels, the centre was mainly English, whilst the rear was brought up by a mixed force of both nationalities. Herbert signalled his captains to bear down in line abreast and engage.

Unfortunately the van came into French range long before the rest, and received heavy punishment from Tourville's broadsides. Herbert kept his main body at extreme range, hoping to surround the French rear division, and in fact made scant contribution to the battle. The brunt was borne by the greatly outnumbered van and rear. The French noted Herbert's error, and manoeuvred so as to engage his leading ships on both sides. Dutch loses soared.

An Allied disaster was in the making, when the wind suddenly dropped. Tourville tried to tow his ships back into action, but the strong ebb-tide thwarted his best endeavours, and his fleet drifted out of range. The Allies dropped anchor whilst keeping full sail set, and were thus able to hold their position. When the tide turned again at 9 pm, Herbert's only thought was to disengage eastwards. Tourville's pursuit was clumsy, and Herbert reached the Thames safely.

This battle cost the Anglo-Dutch fleet a dozen ships, mostly driven ashore and set on fire. The French lost no vessels. An invasion scare gripped England, but all French attention was concentrated on Ireland where William III had just won the Battle of the Boyne. Herbert was court-martialled for lack of fighting spirit, but was acquitted. The Royal Navy's reputation was understandably low after this defeat, but prestige would be regained at the Battle of La Hogue.

THE BOYNE

Williamite War in Ireland

Two Kings Meet in Battle

1690

James' arrival at Kinsale in March 1689 was acclaimed. Here was a chance to rid Ireland of the English. The presence of 3,000 French troops threatened William's crown and a military expedition became necessary. William raised troops in Holland, Denmark, Germany, Scotland and from the Huguenots. At first he doubted the loyalty of English regiments, but seven joined his force of 3,600.

William left Belfast and James left Dublin on the same day. James reached the River Boyne near the village of Donore. His position was opposite the hamlet of Oldbridge and commanded a deep and wide ford. His Irish troops were positioned on lower slopes near the ford with his experienced French troops behind them on higher slopes. Three miles upstream was a second ford at Rossnaree. Between these fords the river was impassable and a bog protected James from attack. William came into the scene of battle on

11th July and battle began before dawn the next day.

The first action was a river crossing at Rossnaree by the Queen's Regiment, the King's Own, the Somerset Light Infantry and the Welsh Fusiliers. This threat was countered by James' cavalry and some French troops. Next took place an impressive crossing of the Oldbridge ford by Dutchmen and the Huguenots. They waded chest deep across 55 metres of water, under musket fire, to engage the Irish in a fierce melee. At about mid-day William crossed a ford downstream from Oldbridge and arrived in Donore. There he was nearly killed by one of his own men.

The regiments south of the river at Rossnaree decided to cross the bog. They found it very soft and covered with waist-high grass, but were successful. James was organising against the threat when news of William's arrival in Donore and the failure of his Irish troops was received. He took flight, William's losses were about 500, James' were three times that many.

William did not pursue his enemy too vigorously. To capture James would be embarrassing. James was dispirited by the result and left for France. No further attempt was made by him to recover his crown and Ireland remained under British control until independence in the 20th Century.

LA HOGUE

War of the League of Augsburg/Nine Years War

Louis XVI's Invasion Prevented

1692

The French navy's defeat at La Hogue was a decisive victory for British seapower in the War of the League of Augsburg (1689-1697). It prevented Louis XVI's proposed invasion of Britain to restore the Catholic James II to the throne in place of the Protestant rulers, William and Mary. Furthermore, British naval dominance in the war was assured.

Louis XVI misjudged the fighting spirit of the Anglo-Dutch fleet, thinking that they could be swept away from his planned invasion route. But the Allied fleet off Spithead was much different from the ill-prepared navy routed two years previously at Beachy Head (1690). They now had discipline, good morale and thirsted for revenge. Overconfidently, Louis ordered Admiral Comte de Tourville with only 44 ships of the line into action against 63 English ships under Admiral Edward Russell and 36 Dutch ships commanded by Philips van Almonde.

Tourville, France's greatest tactician, realised he could not win even as the two fleets sailed alongside each other at Barfleur (near Cherbourg). Russell grasped the initiative, ordering Vice-Admiral Carter and Rear Admiral Shovell to break the French line and attack from both sides. Tourville, using all his 30 years of experience, fought a rearguard action and looked for a moment to flee. Towards evening the tide turned and Tourville swiftly disengaged, having lost 15 ships, including his flagship, *Soleil Royal*.

Russell pursued his foe hotly; Tourville's only chance lay in escaping through the dangerous 'Race of Alderney' between the island and the mainland. The gamble nearly succeeded: all but 13 ships slipped through. These anchored under the guns of St. Vaast, near La Hogue. After waiting and watching for four days, the Allied fleet swept in on a flood tide and audaciously succeeded in burning them all. A detachment of French cavalry, riding into the shallows to help, were unhorsed by Allied sailors using boathooks.

This Anglo-Dutch victory wrested naval superiority from the French fleet, which had been so carefully built up by Jean-Baptiste Colbert. Though the French navy continued to harass and raid Britain's coastline was now safe from invasion. Most importantly for the future, the British rulers, William and Mary, were able to build without hindrance the navy which was to play such a vital role in the future.

STEINKIRK

War of the League of Augsburg/Nine Years War

Luxembourg Defeats William III

1692

The ablest French commander during the later years of Louis XVI's long reign was Francois Henri de Montmorency-Bouteville, Duc de Luxembourg (1628-95). A popular, highly competent and ruthless soldier, he earned the nickname of *la tapissier de Notre Dame*, from the large number of captured enemy colours and standards he sent back to Paris to adorn the cathedral during the Nine Years War (1688-97).

His main opponent was William III the determined opponent of Louis XIV's territorial ambitions. Unfortunately 'Dutch William's' military skills did not equal his abilities as a statesman and a constitutional monarch, as events during the 1692 campaign in the Spanish Netherlands demonstrated.

The French had taken the initiative, besieging and taking Namur in June, before advancing towards Hal so as to threaten Brussels. On the 31st July the French army of 81 battalions, 215 squadrons and 40 guns was camped between Steinkirk on the River Senne and the town of Enghein. Unbeknown to Luxembourg, William III was already planning to force a battle, marching his 61 battalions and 117 squadrons from Liege to near Hal. To attack the 60,000 French with only 40,000 was to take a great risk, but William counted on securing surprise. Using a planned spy to persuade the French that he was advancing on Ninove, where the open terrain would favour cavalry action, William in fact intended to attack the French right-wing near Steinkirk by advancing overnight along the Senne valley, despite the very broken nature of the countryside which made movement difficult, pretending this move was only a foraging expedition.

Luxembourg was greatly surprised to find his right wing attacked at dawn on 3rd August by 15,000 troops, but although his available men suffered many casualties amidst the walls and hedgerows, the Swiss Guards won enough time for the French Household troops to be brought up. General MacKay and his regiments of tiring English infantry found themselves strongly counter-attacked, and after a desperate hand-to-hand fight the weight of French numbers began to tell. The final blow was delivered by Boufflers' dragoons against the English flank, and at midday William ordered a retreat. His gamble cost him 8,500 casualties, including many English troops, but the French had lost all of 7,000 men.

BREST

War of the League of Augsburg/Nine Years War

A Surprise That Failed

1694

In 1694 King William III ordered a raid on the French naval base of Brest, the intention being to destroy shipping and create a furore that would distract Louis XIV's troops from Flanders to defend their north coast. The task was entrusted to General Talmash and 7,000 troops, who were to be convoyed by Admiral Russell's Anglo-Dutch fleet in June.

There is clear evidence that the plan was betrayed to the French authorities well in advance, and there has been much speculation about the identity of the informant. One such suspect was John Churchill, later Duke of Marlborough, who indubitably was in touch occasionally with the court-in-exile King James II at Saint Germain, but the evidence that he was in fact the author of the Camaret Bay letter is inconclusive, as much of the information is conflicting and some is clearly fabricated. So the implication of the future Duke appears to have been the work of his political enemies,

Marlborough already being in disgrace for criticising the royal Dutch favourites.

Admiral Russell embarked 12 regiments of foot and two of marines at Portsmouth, and set sail down the Channel in early June. On the 6th Russell detached Rear-Admiral Berkeley's squadron with the transport vessels off Brest Roads, and sailed on with the remainder of the fleet for the Mediterranean as he had been ordered

The next day the transports stood in towards Camaret Bay, and Talmash called a council=of-war. The advice of Lord Cutts that a reconnaissance party should be put ashore to test the defences and the degree of French readiness was rejected, and the landing was ordered for the next morning. Early on 8th June the naval vessels engage the forts, whilst Talmash led 1,500 infantry towards the shore in ships' boats. As soon as these grounded, the troops were violently attacked by superior French infantry and cavalry, and Talmash himself was severely hurt in the leg. The landing party had been made upon an ebb-tide few of the boats could be re-floated, and almost every man was killed or taken prisoner. The discomfited survivors sailed back to Portsmouth, which was reached on 12th June, Talmash soon after died of his wound. Thus ended a disastrous enterprise, which led to much public criticism in Parliament and elsewhere.

VIGO

War of Spanish Succession

Skill and Daring Rewarded

1702

The Battle of Vigo was one of the Anglo-Dutch navy's infrequent successes in the War of Spanish Succession (1702-13). Luck, skill and valour all contributed to it.

After returning from the abortive expedition against Cadiz, the Anglo-Dutch fleet was moving up the Spanish coast when suddenly an excited rumour ran around the squadrons. Captain Hardy had learnt that a Spanish fleet, laden with the treasure of the Spanish monarchy, if not with the fortunes of the whole House of Bourbon, was hiding near by.

The rumour proved true – 15 Spanish galleons (178 guns total), guarded by 15 French men-of-war (929 guns), were already unloading their precious cargo in the heavily-protected deep harbour in Vigo Bay. The bay itself, in northern Spain, runs inland (eastwards) some 20 miles. Vigo town, 13 miles in, dominates the approach to the harbour of La Redondela. The harbour entrance, only 800 metres wide, was reinforced with a fort to the south and batteries on either side. Across the mouth stretched a boom which was made out of barrels, ropes and spars, and measured some ten metres in circumference.

On 11th October, Sir George Rooke, the British Admiral, briefed the fleet, then, approaching under cover of mist, disembarked 5,000 men to silence the land resistance. Next day the fort flew the British flag, showing the army had captured it.

Immediately the *Torbay* with 24 others under full sail charged the boom. A crash at full speed brought down all the *Torbay*'s sails as she parted the barrier – though now she was left helpless at the mercy of the guns of five French men-of-war and set ablaze by a fire-ship. As the flames caught the sails lying on the decks, the fire-ship's cargo of snuff suddenly exploded, miraculously extinguishing the flames.

With the allied force surging through the gap, the French commander tried to burn the ships before they fell into enemy hands. But the British were too fast and captured 13 men-of-war as well as several treasure galleons containing doubloons and cargo worth over £2 million.

The success of Vigo was a great boost to Anglo-Dutch morale and finances. It was a bitter blow to the Spanish and French.

BLENHEIM

War of Spanish Succession

A Tactical Masterpiece

1704

The victory over the French and Bavarians at Blenheim showed that Marlborough was not only the finest military mind of his day, but also a consummate diplomat. Forced to share the leadership of the allied forces of Britain and Holland with the defensively-motivated Dutch commanders, he overcame the crippling inertia of his less capable and timid allies with diplomatic genius and tactical skill.

The French King, Louis XIV, was preparing armies in Italy and along the Rhine to advance on Vienna, with the intention of forcing Austria out of the war and keeping Bavaria on his side.

Knowing that the Dutch would not leave their borders for Vienna, Marlborough had to deceive the Dutch and the French simultaneously. Leaking the intelligence that he planned to attack France through the Moselle, he moved off slowly. By ingenious feints he duped the French and allayed the

Dutch fears.

Suddenly he abandoned his cover and by well-organised forced marches reached the Danube, where he joined the Austrian army of Prince Eugene. By 12th August, his army, 54,000 strong, was facing the Franco-Bavarian forces (65,000 men) across the River Nebel. Although the forces were evenly matched, Marlborough quickly saw that the French cavalry, ranged in the centre of the four-mile battle line behind the marshy Nebel, was too far away from the river to be really useful. The British commander, by positioning his infantry centrally with cavalry behind, was able by mid-afternoon (13th August) to cross the river and split the French centre with alternate cavalry and infantry charges.

At the same time, Brigadier-General Rowe's British Brigade checked Marshal Tallard's infantry on the allied left at the village of Blenheim. With incredible bravery they advanced until their brigadier could actually stick his sword into the village's palisade before opening their fore. Then they held their ground resolutely. Meanwhile Eugene's forces kept the French left fully occupied.

Tallard, forced continually to weaken his centre in reinforcing the flanks, gave Marlborough the chance to end what was turning into a bloody stalemate. Gathering his cavalry together, Marlborough ordered a charge of such power that the French centre crumbled, exposing the nine supporting battalions to the irresistible fury of the Allies; the infantry in Blenheim was forced to surrender.

RAMILLIES

War of Spanish Succession

Marlborough's Decisive Victory

1706

One of the most decisive battles fought by the British army in the War of the Spanish Succession took place on Whit Sunday, 23rd May 1706, not far from Namur. Marlborough and 62,000 British and allied troops unexpectedly encountered the camp of Marshal Villeroi's 60,000 French in a dense morning mist, and decided to attack.

The French position stretched for four miles, protected by the River Mehaigne on its right and by the marshes of the Little Ghete before its left wing. By one o'clock Marlborough had drawn up his men along a three-mile-line facing the French, and after an hour-long bombardment by his 120 cannon he launched two exploratory attacks. Near the Mehaigne, the Dutch Guards soon tumbled the French from two forward villages, whilst away to the north General Orkney's 12 British battalions supported by cavalry managed to cross the marshes. Villeroi, who had received orders from Louis XIV to watch the place where the redcoats first attacked, moved up reinforcements from his centre near Ramillies, unaware that he was thus playing Marlborough's game.

Realising that the battle would have to be won near Ramillies and to the south of it, Marlborough began to transfer cavalry from his right, down a convenient valley, unseen by the French. He then launched Overkirk's Dutch cavalry against the horsemen forming Villeroi's right. A huge cavalry action of varying fortunes commenced. At one crisis Marlborough intervened in person to rally the Dutch, and was only saved from death or capture by his devoted trumpeter as he struggled free from his slain horse. As he remounted the officer holding his stirrup was killed by a ball that passed between Marlborough's legs. But then reinforcements arrived from the right, and the French cavalry were flung back until they were forming a line of right-angles to their main position.

After pulling Orkney back and secretly transferring half his men through the hidden valley, Marlborough launched his infantry against Ramillies village forming the hinge of the French line. Villeroi's army broke and fled – and were immediately pursued far into the night. The Marshal had lost 19,000 men and 50 cannon; Marlborough's losses were under 5,000. Exploiting this great victory, by September Marlborough was master of most of modern Belgium.

OUDENARDE

War of Spanish Succession

Marlborough's Bold Victory

1708

Oudenarde rallied the morale of the Grand Alliance after a series of disasters which had lasted throughout 1707 and into 1708. The Duke of Marlborough was very despondent until he was joined by Prince Eugene (but not the Imperial Army) at Aasche on 9th July. Heartened by the Prince's robust confidence, Marlborough devised a bold plan to defeat Vendome's army of 85,000 men as it prepared to besiege Oudenarde. On the night of 10th July the Anglo-Dutch army (80,000 strong) made a forced march to surprise the French next morning.

The ensuing engagement was more of a contact action than a set-piece battle. Marlborough took a great risk when he ordered the main body of the army to follow Major-General Cadogan's advance guard over the Scheldt half-way between the town and French forces deploying behind the River Norken, but the gamble succeeded.

At first the French were too surprised to react, and the Duke profited from this to hurry fresh battalions over the pontoon bridges. He was aided by dissension between the French commanders – Vendone and Burgundy – which resulted in half their force never joining battle; this gave Marlborough just enough time to reinforce Cadogan sufficiently. A bitter and fluctuating struggle developed around the villages of Eyne, Heurne and Groenewald which lasted from 3 pm to nightfall. The Duke was always at hand with new units to extend the Allied battle line as fresh French formations entered the fray, whilst Prince Eugene commanded the right and centre.

Infuriated by Burgundy's intransigence, Vendome forgot his role as Commander-in-Chief and plunged into the fighting, half-pike in hand. Judging his moment with customary skill, Marlborough sent General Overkirk and the young Prince of Orange on a long, concealed detour through Oudenarde to the Boser Couter heights. Unnoticed by the French, this led to a decisive attack on the enemy flank and rear, whilst Eugene led a desperate charge against their left. By 8 pm half the French army was surrounded, but the Allies were forced to call a halt in the drkness and many Frenchmen escaped. Nevertheless, 15,000 French fell or were captured; the Allied loss was 4,000. French morale was shattered, and the victory led to the recapture of Ghent and Bruges and to the fall of Lille, second city of France.

MALPLAQUET

War of Spanish Succession

Marlborough's Hardest Victory

1709

Five years of campaigning in the Spanish Netherlands had brought the armies of the Grand Alliance within sight of the French frontier, and by September 1709 only the fortress of Mons stood between them and the road to Paris. A siege was opened on the 9th of that month.

Louis XIV, aware of what was at stake, ordered Marshal Villars to take any risk to save the fortress, and sent Marshall Boufflers to join him in command of the dispirited French army. Villars set out to court battle, but with barely 80,000 men and 60 guns he wisely chose a strong position for his stand to the north of Malplaquet. Placing his wings in two dense woods, he fortified the intervening gap and massed his cavalry in the rear. Barely 10 miles south of Mons, he knew that the Allies would take the bait, and advance to attack.

On 10th September Marlborough and Prince Eugen of Savoy marched from near Mons, and began to deploy their 110,000 men and 100 guns facing the French. Confident of their ability to destroy Villars at their leisure, they postponed their opening attack until the following day. Their plan was hardly subtle: heavy attacks against the French flanks would weaken the centre, through which the Allied cavalry would charge to complete the victory. Villars, meanwhile, entrusted his right wing to Boufflers, and completed his defences.

At 8am on 11th September, the Allies launched preliminary attacks, but for some time made little progress. The Allied right wing penetrated the Wood of Taisnieres at heavy host, while on their left the Dutch attacks against Boufflers were massacred by a cunningly-sited battery. About midday, however, Allied troops began to emerge from Taisieres Wood, and this induced Villars to move troops from his centre. At 1 pm Lord Orkney occupied the weakened redoubts, and 30,000 Allied cavalry surged through the intervals. A tremendous cavalry battle ensued and Villars fell wounded. The Allies came off best, but were too exhausted to exploit it, and Boufflers retired in good order. Marlborough had lost a terrible 24,000 casualties to the French 12,000 killed and wounded.

Both sides claimed a victory, but French morale soared whilst Marlborough's reputation sustained a telling blow. Mons duly fell, but the war continued until 1713.

DETTINGEN

War of the Austrian Succession

The Mouse Trap

1743

In the spring of 1743 King George II of Great Britain and the Earl of Stair marched into Germany from the Netherlands with a mixed army of British, Hanoverians and Austrians. The intention was to cross the Main southwards to the middle Rhine and so threaten France, under Duke of Noailles, that they could offer no assistance to the other French Army retreating from Bohemia.

Unfortunately King George II delayed and by June 1743 he found that the French had seized the initiative and crossed the right bank of the Main above and below the Allied army in a mouse-trap.

French held the left bank of the Main with artillery, and no retreat was possible through the heavily wooded hills on the farther side.

The only way out for the troops was to force a passage north-westwards through the narrow gap to Hanau where provisions were available. George attempted to do this on the 27th June, and by midday a line formed facing the French under Grammont, who barred the way in front of the village of Dettingen.

Noailles himself was upstream, ready to fall on the Allies' flank and rear as soon as they had been repulsed at Dettingen. But Noailles had failed to reckon with the indiscipline in the French Army. Grammont had moved too far forward, and was in front of the ravine running into the Main at Dettingen and not, as he should have been, behind it. The position which the troops had to attack was therefore, though difficult, not desperate. The crushing platoon fire of the British infantry rolled forth, and the French infantry in the centre suffered severely. The French cavalry then charged the British left, which had been heavily enfiladed by the French guns from across the river, and a desperate struggle ensued, in which the British cavalry, particularly the 3rd Dragoons and infantry, later known as the Royal Scots Fusiliers and the Royal Welch Fusiliers in turn, gradually forced the French back. A final cavalry charge against the British right also failed.

Now a general advance thrust the French back on their bridges to the left flank; large numbers were drowned fording the stream, and the way of escape was clear. George gladly took it, Hanue was reached and the King returned to England. Dettingen would become the last battle in which a British sovereign commanded his troops in a pitched battle.

FONTENOY

War of the Austrian Succession

Great Courage and High Casualties

1745

The Battle of Fontenoy took place on 11th May 1745 during the War of the Austrian Succession. France and Russia had attempted to obtain control of Austrian territory, and Britain and Holland had gone to the assistance of the Austrians.

In the early stages the war went well for Britain and led to the resounding victory at Dettingen in 1743. Subsequently, political ineptitude in England caused a dangerous relaxation in the resolve to bring the war to a satisfactory conclusion.

At the same time Marshal de Saxe, the French Commander-in-Chief, was displaying exceptional military foresight, drive and talent. He was not a Frenchmen by birth, and the army he commanded was generally inefficient; however, he handled it with masterly skill.

The Allied Commander, the Duke of Cumberland (son of George II), was less talented but was respected by his men. Unfortunately he was no diplomat and was at loggerheads with the Dutch Commander Count Waldeck.

In April 1745 Saxe's army aimed to take Tournai, in Belgium. When Cumberland came up to prevent this, he was confronted with a system of trenches and strongpoints (known at the time as redoubts), manned by 70,000 troops at the village of Fontenoy. The rear was protected by the river by the river Scheldt. With 15,000 less men he decided on a frontal attack, although his numbers were hopelessly inadequate for the task. Neither his Dutch nor his Austrian troops could make any headway but the British element, showing superb discipline and courage, forced an entry into the French line near the village of Fontenoy. Saxe counter-attacked with cavalry charges but they were repulsed and the British once more pressed forward. Finally Saxe threw in his Irish Brigade (Catholic mercenaries), consisting of six battalions, and these fresh troops checked the British advance. Cumberland ordered a general withdraw. Casualties were very high on all sides. Reinforcements for the Allied force could not be provided and Saxe was able to capture Tournai, Ghent and Ostend. However, all these conquests were restored in the subsequent Peace of Aix-la-Chapelle (Aachen) in 1748.

For an attack on a prepared defensive position a numerical superiority of at least three to one is considered necessary. Cumberland ignored this military concept.

PRESTONPANS

Jacobite Rising

English Routed by Highlanders

1745

On 16th September 1745, the Jacobite army, with Bonnie Prince Charles at its head, entered Edinburgh to proclaim the Old Protector, king, in place of 'yon German lairdie', George II. Meanwhile Lieutenant-General Sir John Cope, commander of the army in Scotland, was hurrying down from Inverness. Landing at Dunbar on 17th September, he was on the road to Edinburgh two days later with an army of 3,000 men. News of Cope's progress reached Charles, who set out, with his 2,500 Highlanders, to meet him.

On the morning of 20th September, when warned of the Jacobite approach, Cope speedily took up a position north of the Preston-Seton road, near the village of Prestonpans. The ground was well chosen, flanked by a 3.7 metre wall to the west, and protected by a marsh in front.

That night, the Jacobite leaders met on the high ground across the march. Lord George Murray's plan to march around the eastern end of the bog met with approval. Better still, a local man, Robert Anderson, offered to take them across the morass itself, by a track he used when snipe shooting. At 4 am the Highland army moved off.

Cope, sensing something amiss, redeployed his army at right angles to its old position to face the new threat. The infantry was massed in the centre, with the dragoons on either wing, but they were barely in position before the Highlanders were upon them.

Cope's seaman gunners fled in panic as the clansmen charged 'with a hideous noise'. Those left to man the artillery inflicted some damage with a hasty salvo, but the Highlanders quickly recovered and charged again. The cavalry, thrown into confusion, bolted, leaving the horrified infantry to sustain the full weight of the Highland onslaught. Soon they began to waver, and despite Cope's valiant efforts to rally his army the battle was over in 15 minutes: it had cost the English some 1,000 casualties.

According to Prince Charles, whose spelling is notorious, 'Only our first line had occasion to engaje, for actually in five minutes ye yield was clired of ye Enemy... we only losed a hundred men... ye army afterwards had a fine plunder'. Those who were not hacked to pieces fled to Berwick-on-Tweed.

Cope's defeat was a severe shock to the Government. It sealed the Jacobite hold on almost all Scotland, but it gave Charles fatal confidence in the ability of his clansman.

CULLODEN

Jacobite Rising

The Final Defeat of the Rebellion

1746

The Battle of Culloden on 16th April 1746 was the final defeat of the Jacobite rebellion. The Jacobite army under the 'Young Pretender', Charles Edward Stuart, had returned from their foray into England, defeated the English at Falkirk, and returned to the Inverness region where they occupied the town and surroundings. The army encamped on Culloden Moor to await the pursuing English army under the Duke of Cumberland, son of George II.

Charles army numbered 7,000 and were a ragbag mixture of Scots, Irish and French who argued among themselves and were virtually untrained while the English 8,000 troops were trained and disciplined.

The Jacobite faced the government forces on a narrow dense front with the Water of Naim about half-a-mile to their right. The left wing, anchored on the Culloden Parks walls, was under the command of the Duke of Perth. His brother, John Drummond, commanded the centre, while Lieutenant-General Lord George Murray commanded the right wing which was flanked by the Culwhiniac enclosure walls.

The Governemt forces were drawn up in three lines. The first line was under the Earl of Albemarle, second line under General Major-General John Huske whilst the third line were held in reserve.

The battle began approximately at 1 pm with an artillery bombardment from the government Redcoats which pummelled the crowded rebels. Shortly afterwards Charles Stuart issued the order for the Highlanders to advance. The right of the Jacobites was hit hard by a volley of musketry from the Redcoats. The left flank advanced more slowly, hampered by boggy ground and further to cover, they took heavy casualties. Many of the Highlanders managed to charge and breach the government first line but were caught by the musket fire and hard hand-to-hand fighting with great ferocity of the government second line. New Redcoat tactic of bayoneting the exposed side of the man to the right, rather than confronting the one directly in front appeared to have paid dividends.. The Highlanders finally broke and fled.

The whole battle lasted less than an hour. Prince Charles rode away and the clan regiments left the field. Their retreat being covered by the Irish Pickets, as well as other regular regiments of foot.

Jacobite casualties were estimated at 1,500-2,000 killed or wounded to Cumberland's 50 dead and 259 wounded.

In the weeks that followed many of the survivors were hunted down and killed. Charles managed to evade capture and escaped to France and exile.

ARCOT

Second Carnatic War

A Staunch Defence Wins the Carnatic

1751

Anglo-French rivalry for predominance over the Deccan and Carnatic areas of India was bitter and protracted. Benefiting from a civil war between Indian princes, French troops under Duplex joined Chunda Sahib's army, and tightly besieged Trichinopoly, where Mahomet Ali, the British candidate for the vice-royalty of the Deccan, had taken refuge, together with the main forces of the East India Company.

Robert Clive, aged 25 years was a junior merchant of the company. He boldly proposed to lead a skeleton force to make a diversion against Chunda Sahib's capital, Arcot, on the River Palar. He knew that Chunda's army was 200 miles away, and calculated that even a small success near Arcot would trigger off a revolt against the absent ruler.

Governor Saunders approved the daring plan, and on 26th August Clive set off at the head of 210 European and 300 sepoy troops – practically the last resources of the British East India Company.

This tiny force and their three field guns approached Arcot on 1st September, and the garrison fled at their approach. With feverish haste Clive set about gathering provisions and repairing the neglected fortifications. A series of skirmishes fought beyond the town scattered the nearest Indian troops, but the Chunda's son, Raja Sahib, was near Arcot by mid-September with 4,000 men, aided by a French detachment.

Clive's defence of the fort of Arcot was masterly. Despite a harrowing and destructive fire from the French guns, he held the position; but casualties were mounting and his defences were crumbling fast. October passed with no diminution in the tiny garrison's morale, and hearing that a relief force was on its way, Raja Sahib decided on an all-out assault. His plan was betrayed to Clive, who calmly disposed his 80 remaining European and 120 sepoy troops. At dawn on 14th November the attack began: Armoured elephants attacked the gates of the citadel, but a volley sent them charging back through their own ranks. An assault on the breaches also foundered' and after an hour the attack petered out with the loss of 400 casualties. Only six of Clive's garrison had fallen. Next day, Raja Sahib abandoned the siege after 50 fruitless days, his retreat compelled by the approach of a relief force from Madras. Clive had won a victory that would prove to be a turning point in the British conquest of India.

CAPE BRETON/
LOUISBOURG

Seven Years War

Struggle for the Colonies

1758

The Seven Years War, which lasted from 1756 to 1763, was fought partly in Europe and partly in Canada and India. The French were strongly entrenched in North America and planned to extend their overlordship from New Orleans in the south to Nova Scotia in the north. Fighting had already begun before the war was declared between England and France in 1756, but the English settlers, protected by George Washington and the Colonel Militia, and General Braddock with the regular army, fared badly against their French rivals. Soon the French General, Montcalm, captured several important outposts from the British and it appeared as if further successes were now within the French grasp.

However, General Amherst now set out to reduce French power. As a first step he determined to capture Cape Breton, of which the capital was the town of Louisburg. Amherst was accompanied by Admiral Boscawen, who conveyed 12,000 men in 157 ships. They were mainly Scots. Among them was the future General Wolfe who was at that time a Colonel.

The harbour was strongly defended and, to make it even more difficult to attack, the French sank three of their frigates in the entrance. Fog delayed the British convoy, then high winds and rough surf made landing very difficult. The landing party was divided into three divisions, the one on the left being commanded by Wolfe. The French held their fire until the British were close in, then directed concentrated volleys on to the occupants of the landing craft. Wolfe's was the first party to get ashore but after heavy casualties the other divisions followed. This was on 11th June. The weather was so bad that progress to Louisburg, even miles away, was very slow and ships could not unload necessary stores until it settled. However, by the 19th the British had managed to bring up guns and lay siege to Louisburg, Strenuous fighting continued for a week, when the town surrounded.

In spite of the heavy fighting British casualties were fewer than expected, the number killed being 525. Among them was the Duke of Dundonald who had taken a leading part in repelling a French sortie. The gains were very considerable, for they included large numbers of arms in addition to this valuable strategic base.

THE HEIGHTS OF ABRAHAM

The Seven Years War

The Battle for Quebec

1759

At the beginning of the Seven Years' War in 1756, the British Prime Minister had outlined as one of his objectives the capture of the French possessions in North America. In 1758 the British succeeded in capturing several important forts in French Canada, but it was not until 1759 that an expedition was launched to take Quebec, which guarded that part of the St. Lawrence where the river narrowed to the width of a mile. The expeditionary force was 8,000 strong and commanded by General James Wolfe.

Conveyed by a fleet under Admiral Saunders, the expeditionary force arrived on the 25th June 1759 off the Isle of Orleans opposite Quebec, Wolfe's combined force was unable to make much progress against Quebec, as the fortified town perched on a rocky bluff, surrounded by cliffs and steep gorges.

Throughout July and August the British besieged Quebec and launched one unsuccessful assault. In some desperation Wolfe and Saunders decided to convoy some 5,000 men up river. Under the cover of a bombardment by the remainder of the force, these men would attempt to scale the bluffs and assault Quebec from the rear. In the early hours of the 13th September this plan was successfully put into operation, and the French commander at Quebec learnt that the British had scaled the bluffs and were deploying on the Plain of Abraham.

The French defenders hastily deployed onto the Plain, and by 9 o'clock the two armies faced each other in the drizzling rain. Fortunately for Wolfe, the French commander, Montcalm, decided to attack immediately instead of waiting for reinforcements. A little later, the French, superior in numbers, advanced to attack, stopping from time to time to fire a volley at the stationary British line. Not until they were 35 metres away did Wolfe give the command to fire, and then there burst forth at point-blank range a murderous volley, a triumph of discipline and fire control. The French wavered and fell into disorder, and Wolfe gave the order to the British regiments to charge. At this moment Wolfe was mortally wounded, but the British charge completely broke the French line, and in a state of wild confusion the French fled the field, bearing with the mortally wounded Montcalm.

As a result of the British success the French retreated and five days later Quebec capitulated.

QUIBERON BAY

The Seven Years War

Victory for Admiral Hawke

1759

During the Seven Years War Britain and France fought in Europe, in their colonies and on the sea. The French considered that the best way of winning the war was to invade England and for that purpose had assembled an invasion fleet of Le Havre. Most of the boats were destroyed by a bombardment from Admiral Rodney's ships and this success was followed by Admiral Boscawen's victory off Toulon. However, the French still maintained a large fleet on the coast of Brittany at Brest, commanded by Admiral Conflans.

On the southern coast of Brittany, at Vannes, opposite Quiberon Bay, was an invasion army waiting for the opportunity to cross the Channel. Outside in the Channel, keeping careful watch on the French dispositions, was Admiral Sir Edward Hawke. However, In November the weather was particularly wild and Hawke was forced to take shelter in Torbay on the 9th of that month.

Hawke's temporary absence enabled Conflans to break out of Brest and sail towards Vanners ready to escort the invasion barges. However, he was observed by Hawke's patrols. Hawke determined to destroy the French fleet in spite of the great hazards of weather and navigation. Conflans tried to evade Hawke by going close inshore but was astonished to find the British ships following him. Although two of Hawke's ships ran ashore, most of their crews were saved. In contrast, in the running battle that followed, the French lost seven ships and 2,500. But the victory was not only in terms of mere numbers. It was an effective destruction of a powerful French fleet and a great setback to French invasion plans. For the rest of the war the British were so much in control of these seas that their ships were able to use the Quiberon anchorage and also maintain shore parties there.

Hawke's skill in winning this devastating victory astonished everyone and even the Admiral himself expressed some surprise at his success. The fact that the weather was extremely bad with gales blowing made the task of venturing close in to an unknown enemy coast, among rocks and shoals, all the while being shot at by a powerful and determined enemy, seem like courting disaster. Visibility was very poor throughout the battle but even with that handicap Hawke could probably have destroyed Conflans' entire fleet if the day had been longer.

LAGOS

Seven Years War

Admiral Boscawen's Last Victory

1759

The Bay of Lagos is a small anchorage on the south coast of Portugal, in the Algarve. In 1759 it saw the crushing defeat of a French squadron, which had been hotly pursued by a British naval force.

A French Commander, de la Clue, blockaded in Toulon with 12 ships, saw his chance to escape when the British Admiral Edward Boscawen, 'Old Dreadnought', was compelled to withdraw his ships to Gibraltar for repair and refitting. The Frenchman planned to sail unnoticed through the Straits of Gibraltar, around the coast of Portugal and thence to Brest. There he would join the French fleet mustering to invade Britain.

The experienced British Admiral placed two look-out ships for just this eventuality: one of them spotted the French at nightfall on 17th August, sailing stealthily along the North African coast, and alerted Boscawen. Though unprepared, the British crews worked keenly all night to refit their ships and soon pursued hotly.

Next morning, when Boscawen sighted seven French ships, they seemed almost unreachable. Fortunately, de la Clue mistook the British for five ships he had lost during the darkness. The instant he realised his mistake, he clapped on all canvas and raced westward for the safety of Portugal's neutral shores.

Slowly but surely, Boscawen gained on the French and eventually, at Cape Lagos, his flagship overhauled the rear enemy ship, the *Centaur*. Ignoring the *Centaur's* broadsides, Boscawen doggedly pursued the *Ocean*, the French flagship. All the other British ships, firing as they passed, crippled the *Centaur*.

Boscawen turned on the *Ocean* with a fearsome broadside, during which de la Clue was severely wounded. The French, fighting desperately, returned murderous volleys which crippled Boscawen's flagship, the *Namur*. Transferring to the *Newark*, he continued his vigorous pursuit.

Four French ships fled into Lagos Bay and sought refuge under the walls of the neutral Portuguese forts. Alas for their hopes, the Portuguese gave no help. Consequently the British ships were able to sail in and capture two of the French ships and burn two others, on the morning of 19th August.

In this battle the British lost 56 killed and 196 wounded. By contrast, 100 French were killed and 70 wounded on the *Ocean* alone. Admiral Boscawen's career thus ended triumphantly.

WANDIWASH

Seven Years War

British Triumph in India

1760

The Seven Years War saw great Anglo-French colonial rivalry in India. Clive's victory at Plassey (1757) gained the East India Company virtual control of Bengal, but the struggle around Madras remained fluid. Although the French commander, Count Lally, failed to take Madras itself, he remained master over much of the Carnatic, and the British authorities were determined to regain the region and defeat French pretensions in India once and for all.

Wandewash's capture would drive a wedge halfway between the French bases of Pondicherry and Arcot. In September 1759, Major Brereton attempted a storming but was repulsed. The arrival of Colonel Eyre Coote with reinforcements led to another attempt, and on 29th November Wandewash surrendered. Lally at once gathered his scattered and somewhat demoralised forces, and on 14th January, 1760 he marched from Trivatone fully determined to retake the town.

Learning of the French intention, Coote marched from the Madras area, intending both to save his garrison and bring the French to a decisive battle. Early on the 22nd, after some preliminary manoeuvring, the armies met east of Wandewash. Lally deployed 2,250 European, 1,300 Sepoy troops and 16 guns in a single battle-line near his camps, leaving 500 men to besiege the town.

Coote drew up his 1,980 British soldiers, 1,300 Sepoys, 1,250 native irregular horse and 16 guns in three lines, and advanced to contact. French cavalry soon caused the irregular horsemen to flee, but the single British squadron and two guns retrieved the situation. Finding Lally advancing his three French regiments, Coote halted and opened musketry fire. The rival lines engaged at 1 pm. On Coote's left the French made a short-lived breakthrough but were then repulsed. On the British left a lucky shot exploded French ammunition waggons in an entrenchment, for which a desperate fight developed. Eventually Major Brereton stormed it, but was shot down. British guns then routed Lally's regiment, and the remaining French retreated, burning their camp and abandoning the siege. Lally lost 600 men and 24 guns, whilst Coote lost 187. French power in the Carnatic soon collapsed, and on 15th January 1761 Pondicherry surrendered. Lally was recalled in disgrace to France, and executed. British influence in India was now paramount.

BUNKER HILL

American War of Independence

General Gage's Costly Victory

1775

Bunker Hill, which overlooks Boston from a peninsula across the Charles River, was the site of the first battle in the American War of Independence. The colonists eventually lost the encounter against the British, but fought so well that their morale was greatly raised for the struggles ahead.

In 1775 all Massachusetts stood in revolt against the British garrison in Boston. During the night of the 16th June, a detachment under Colonel Prescott seized the initiative by fortifying Breed's Hill (on the lower slopes of Bunker Hill). At dawn, the British commander, General Gage saw the threat. However, instead of ordering his fleet to isolate the peninsula, he despatched 2,300 troops under General Howe, to land and take the well-entrenched American position by an uphill assault.

Howe's troops disembarked near Charlestown. Immediately they met musket fire from the town and the hill, but covered by cannonades from the fleet, which set fire to Charlestown, and by the Boston artillery, they formed lines of attack. They gradually advanced up the steep slope through deep, coarse grass, exposed to the sun's heat in their heavy scarlet uniforms and weighed down with three days rations. The British lines provided simple targets for the American sharp-shooters behind the fort's barricades and fencing stuffed with hay and brush.

Twice the well-drilled British stormed Breed's Hill; twice they were forced back by determined defence. But finally Prescott's men ran short of ammunition. When the British were 30 metres away, the leading rank was devastated with one last salvo, before the defenders retreated pell-mell to their mainland camp at Cambridge.

Quickly the British re-formed and took the fort. They chased and harried the retreating Americans, but did not press their advantage. They had won victory, but at what cost: over 1,000 British casualties against less than 400 American. British tactics had proved to be unsound, the commanders incompetent. The colonists, though ill-armed, were tenacious fighters suited to guerrilla warfare. Bunker Hill, though a defeat, boosted the Americans' morale, and gave them hope that in the ensuing bitter struggle against British imperial power, their qualities of enterprise and flexibility could eventually bring them victory.

BRANDYWINE

American War of Independence

A Defeat for Washington

1777

In the third year of the American War of Independence, the senior British commander in North America, General Sir William Howe, decided to make the capture of the rebel capital, Philadelphia, his main objective.

The late arrival of reinforcements and supplies from England delayed the opening of operations, and this allowed George Washington to form his new Continental Army and absorb the first foreign aid that was appearing from Europe.

At last, on 23rd July, Howe left New York with 15,000 men and sailed up Chesapeake Bay to Head of Elk in Maryland, intending to advance on Philadelphia from the south. The move surprised Washington, who had anticipated a more direct line of attack, but he just had time to move some 11,000 of the Continental Army over the River Delaware from New Jersey. He took up a defensive position at Chad's Ford on Brandywine Creek, thus interposing his force between Howe and the road to Philadelphia. The forces met on 11th September.

Howe was a professional soldier of great skill. He ascertained that Washington was personally commanding part of his army near Chad's Ford, with a second force under General Sullivan guarding his right flank further upstream, Howe ordered Lt-General Knyphausen to demonstrate with 5,000 men opposite Chad's Ford, held by the American commander Nathaniel Greene, whilst General Cornwallis led 10,000 troops by a circuitous route to an upstream ford near Sconnelltown, with orders to outflank Sullivan and attack him from the rear. This bold manoeuvre went undetected by the Americans and Sullivan was caught by Cornwallis in the act of changing his position. A brief fight, and Sullivan's men were in full retreat. Taken between two fires, the American position was grim, but the situation was in part redeemed by Washington. He managed to extricate two brigades commanded by General Green from the fighting against Knyphausen, and sent them to form a defensive flank to hold off Cornwallis. This move, however, weakened the American left, and soon the whole American army was in full retreat for Chester, covered by General Greene's stalwart rearguard. A minor engagement followed, and on 26th September General Howe occupied Philadelphia.

SIEGE OF GIBRALTAR

American War of Independence

Epic Defence of the Rock

1779-1783

Gibraltar, commanding the entrance to the Mediterranean, has always been one of Britain's most important overseas bases since its capture in 1704. When Spain joined the American War of Independence in June 1779, the fortress was blockaded and preparations made for a siege. From then on Gibraltar's survival depended on the British fleet's ability to ensure reinforcements and supplies. The fortress's commander, General George Elliot, introduced rationing, and to save flour ordered that the troops were no longer to powder their hair. The Spanish made no immediate attempt to storm the defences, but an almost continuous cannonade continued. For months at a time the guns were never totally silent.

Early in 1780 Admiral Rodney brought a supply convoy from England. On the way he defeated French and Spanish squadrons, the fortress then remained isolated, except for occasional blockade runners, for over a year.

In June 1780 the Spaniards sent fire-ships into the harbour but they did no harm to the shipping there. There was still no real attempt at an assault and the garrison's families tried to live as normal a life as possible. In April 1781 Admiral Darby brought another convoy which managed to unload its stores despite several days' bombardment.

During the summer of 1782 a French army reinforced the Spanish and the siege-works were pushed closer to the Rock. In September the great assault began. The Spaniards had prepared floating batteries by converting and strengthening old warships. These came within a thousand metres of the harbour defences and were assisted by gunboats and 300 guns on shore. The defenders fired red-hot shot at the batteries but at first could not penetrate their 'armoured' sides. However, as the bombardment continued nine of the batteries caught fire and were destroyed. Although the attack failed, the town of Gibraltar was flattened, with the remaining inhabitants living in cellars. They were now existing on reduced rations and diseases such as scurvy were common among them.

However, relief was on the way. A fleet under Admiral Howe arrived on 11th October. The transports unloaded their supplies while Howe prevented the more numerous Spanish fleet from interfering. After this the French and Spanish fleets gave up hope of capturing Gibraltar. They began to withdraw their forces and after 43 months the siege ended in January 1783.

YORKTOWN

American War of Independence

Decisive Siege in America

1781

As the American War of Independence entered its sixth year, Charles, Marquis Cornwallis, marched from North Carolina into Virginia, where he reinforced his army to 7,500 men, Despite his decided superiority of force over General Lafayette's command in the area, the British commander turned east in order to reach the coast and thus keep in touch by sea with the British force under General Clinton situated in New York. Cornwallis reached Yorktown on 1st August, and at once set about fortifying the mouth of the York River.

Unfortunately for the British, Admiral de Grasse's French fleet was able to blockade the river, and soon General George Washington was leading half the Continental Army, and the French forces of Rochambeau from the vicinity of New York, to join Lafayette and de Grasse's landing party outside the Yorktown lines. Moving up from Williamsburg, Washington had some 13,000 troops around Yorktown by 28th September, and the siege began. For the defence Cornwallis had about 8,000 men and 65 guns, including a force under Colonel Tarleton holding Gloucester on the north bank of the York River.

By 6th October the allied siege lines and batteries were in place. On the 8th the 52 siege guns began to batter the British defences as the approach trenches and first parallel snaked forward. Two days later the second parallel was begun, but it was soon found that the two British forts – Nos 9 and 10 placed at the south-eastern end of Yorktown's defences – were enfilading the American trenches from the riverbank. Accordingly a successful night-attack was launched against these two posts.

In an attempt to hamper the progress of the siege works, General Cornwallis ordered a strong sortie from his position on the night of the 15th, but by early the next morning this had been repulsed by the watchful Americans. As the enemy guns were moved up closer, Cornwallis asked for an armistice and opened up negotiations for surrender. On 19th October the British troops marched out to lay down their arms, and Tarleton soon followed suit. The siege had cost the British almost 500 casualties, and the Americans and French only 262 killed and wounded. The defeat broke the resolve of the British to hold the American Colonies, and in 1782 peace negotiations, which led to the Treaty of Versailles and the achievement of American Independence, were begun.

CHESAPEAKE BAY

American War of Independence

Navy Fails to Rescue Army

1781

In the summer of 1781 the last British field army in America, under General Cornwallis, was besieged at Yorktown on the coast of Chesapeake Bay. The French and American armies under Rochambeau and Washington had surrounded Cornwallis, but he could still escape or be reinforced by sea. This route was, however, blocked on 30th August when Admiral de Grasse arrived with the French West Indies fleet. Now Cornwallis' only hope was that the British fleet could restore the situation by a decisive victory.

Meanwhile the British West Indies fleet had also come north and joined their New York Squadron under Rear Admiral Graves. On 5th September Graves reached the Chesapeake. He knew nothing of de Grasse's arrival and was looking for a French convoy escorting the Allies' siege artillery to Yorktown. Graves, with 19 ships of the line, found de Grasse, with 24 ships anchored at Lynnhaven Bay, on the southern side of the Chesapeake. De

Grasses set sail but the wind and tide were against him and his fleet had to struggle to pass north of Cape Henry and reach the open sea. This gave Graves an excellent opportunity to attack the leading French ships and eliminate them before the rest could join the battle.

However, this would have meant abandoning the line of battle which was laid down in the British Fighting Instructions. Graves was no Nelson, and could only fight the battle according to the book. While the French struggled out he sailed on into Chesapeake Bay then, reaching shoal water, turned at about 2.30 pm so that he was now sailing east and thus parallel to the French fleet. Graves then hove-to until the leading ships of the two lines were opposite each other, and at last closed on the French.

The leading ships got into action just after 4 pm, but when darkness fell two hours later most of the fleets had not engaged. For three more days Graves remained off Chesapeake, but the French avoided battle, and so he returned to New York to repair his damaged ships.

Graves remained there for a month, sailing again on 19th October. When he reached the Chesapeake he found that Cornwallis had already surrendered. The defeat at Yorktown ended British hopes of holding America, but for a few hours off Cape Henry on the morning of 5th September, history had hung in the balance.

PORTO NOVO

Second Anglo-Mysore War

Hyder Ali Defeated

1781

The complexities of 18th-century politics within the Indian sub-continent were immense. Even the ruthless genius of the great Warren Hasting's, appointed Governor-General over all East India Company possessions by Lord North's Regulating Act of 1773, was hard pressed to keep the interleaved levels of intrigue and conspiracy under some form of control. One major source of trouble was the great Mahratta confederacy of Central India. Another was the long-standing enmity of the native Moslem state of Mysore, which led to four wars between 1767 and 1799 before British paramountcy was established.

The Maharaja of Mysore, Hyder Ali, was an ancient enemy of the East India Company. In his first war, which ended in 1769, he gained a not unfavourable treaty from the Company, but his hatred burnt on. In 1780 he sensed that a combination of circumstances was operating in his favour, and determined on a new effort. News of British military disasters in North America had reached India, whilst the open involvement of France in that struggle implied greater assistance for Indian prepared to challenge the East India Company. Furthermore, Hyder Ali knew that most of Warren Hastings' resources were already committed to the Mahratta war, albeit not to Mysore's interests against that confederacy. Accordingly he opened secret negotiations with the French and then invaded the Carnatic.

To begin with success favoured Hyder's arms. On 10th September 1780 he overwhelmed a small British force at Parambakam, cut it to pieces, and swept on at the head the end of 60,000 men towards the great prize of Madras.

Warren Hastings reacted with commendable speed and energy. Suspending the Governor of Madras, who was not the man to face the crisis, he ordered General Sir Eyre Coote (Commander-in-Chief in India since 1779), an experienced soldier who had fought under Clive at Plassey, to sail from Calcutta with 8,000 mixed British and Sepoy troops to the Carnatic. In successive operations General Coote raised the siege of Wandewash and moved against Hyder Ali's main army. Ignoring a minor setback at Chelhambakam, he caught his opponent at Porto Novo on 1st July 1781 and inflicted a major defeat. The success saved the Madras Presidency, and led to the Second Mysore War ending in 1784.

THE SAINTES

American War of Independence

Britain's Naval Honour Restored

1782

'Fortunes smiles on those who dare'. The decisive British defeat of the French at sea in the Battle of 'The Saintes' clearly illustrates this maxim. The swift thinking and tactical genius of the experienced British Admiral, Sir George Rodney, won a convincing, morale-boosting victory for Britain's forces in the West Indies. For not only were the British about to lose the American War of Independence but valuable possessions in the West Indies were being threatened by the opportunists ambitions of the Colonists' allies: the French and the Spanish. Victory at The Saintes stopped the Franco-Spanish threat, restored Britain's bruised prestige and enabled her to keep most of the Caribbean territories at the Treaty of Versailles in 1763.

On his arrival with the British fleet of 37 ships at St Lucia in December 1781, Rodney realised that the French and Spanish were planning a combined attack on Jamaica. He had learned that the French fleet of 36 ships and 150 merchantmen and 5000 troops were sailing to link up with a strong Spanish fleet at Cape Francois.

Swift and decisive action was needed. Rodney skirmished with the French on 9th April 1782 and then, on the 12th, intercepted them in The Saintes Passage between Dominica and Guadeloupe. In tense silence the two evenly-matched fleets sailed past each other on opposite courses. As the lines drew level, a small shift in wind direction gave the British commander his chance. Two French vessels altered course a fraction and immediately Rodney ordered part of his fleet to sail through each gap, cutting the French line into three parts and enabling the British to isolate their prey.

Rodney's tactical brilliance combined with the acuteness of his captains gave the decisive advantage (this same manoeuvre was later used by Nelson at Trafalgar in 1805). Seeing that he had been outmanoeuvred, the French Admiral, the Comte de Grasses, immediately discontinued the action and sailed off at full speed. Rodney detached a squadron to catch stragglers though he did not pursue vigorously – for which he was criticised by his second in command and for which he was actually replaced as Admiral. He did, however, capture five French ships, including the Comte de Grasse's flagship the *Ville de Paris*, as well as preventing the attack on Jamaica. Moreover he restored Britain's damaged naval prestige.

TOULON

Federalist Revolts

Napoleon Begins his Rise

1793

In 1793, the year of The Terror in France, the country was torn between revolutionary republicans and royalists. As the rabble revolutionary armies ran riot in France, Britain played a negative and indecisive role, lacking the soldiers to exploit their opportunities.

A marvellous chance fell to Admiral Hood as his fleet of 21 ships blockaded the naval arsenal at Toulon, which dominated the Gulfs of Lyons and Genoa and housed the French Mediterranean fleet, including 30 ships of the line. The loyalist inhabitants had just heard of the arson, rape and massacre which had followed the republican Carteaux's capture of Marseilles, 30 miles to the north-west. They appealed to Hood to save them from the hands of the rebels.

Hood sailed in as Carteaux's army marched irresistibly on Toulon, but his joy was short-lived as he realised that he had only 12,000 men – Spaniards,

Austrians, Piedmontese, Neapolitans – plus the inhabitants and too few British troops.

The French army, swelling to 45,000 threatened the walls. An unknown Corsican captain of artillery, one Napoleon Bonaparte, with the cruel eye of the military genius, set to work bombarding the forts to the south-west of the town. As each fort crumbled the revolutionary troops bayed for blood, striking fear deep into the allied hearts. Without British reinforcements the town was doomed, but Britain had no troops to send, aside from a small detachment under General O'Hara, who was immediately captured!

As the shells thundered nearer and nearer, Hood resolved to evacuate all troops and the loyalist townspeople, devastating the town when he left. During a frenzied assault, under cover of a storm on 17th December, Hood instructed Captain Sidney Smith to destroy the French fleet. Thanks to the cowardice of the Neapolitans and the treachery of the Spaniards, only nine ships were burned and four taken away, leaving 17 for the revolutionaries as they swarmed into the town hurling threats and curses on the British fleet, which had slipped out of the harbour only just in time.

Overstretched and underprepared, Britain had to fall back. Among the young captains in Hood's fleet a certain Horatio Nelson swore that one day he would get his revenge.

THE GLORIOUS
FIRST OF JUNE

French Revolutionary War

First Napoleonic Naval Battle

1794

In 1794 France's situation was desperate. Not only was she at war with most of Europe, but famine was threatening. A huge convoy of grain ships had assembled in America, and if it crossed the Atlantic safely would prevent famine and enable France to continue the war. The main French fleet sailed from Brest to protect the convoy. Its commander was Admiral Villaret-Joyeuse who had risen rapidly from the rank of lieutenant after the Revolution.

The British fleet, under Admiral Lord Howe, sailed to look for the convoy. The two fleets met in the Atlantic on 28th May. Howe was then 69 years old but immediately revealed himself as a master of naval tactics. During the next two days he skilfully manoeuvred his fleet into the most advantageous position for an attack, but on the 30th-31st May fog prevented a battle. Next day, 1st June, Howe led his fleet towards the French.

In 18th Century naval tactics the greatest problem was to force a decisive battle. It was difficult to control a battle and accepted tactics and formations were very inflexible. Howe's solution was to order his fleet to approach the French in line abreast, using the advantage of the wind. Then each ship was to pass through the French line and take up position to the leeward, preventing the French from withdrawing. This was a revolutionary idea, and Howe did not expect all his captains to understand the orders. He prophesised that he would capture one French ship for every British ship which broke through and he was right. Six French ships were captured and one sunk. The battle dissolved into a number of short-range actions. The first broadsides from Howe's flagship, *Queen Charlotte*, killed 300 men on board the French flagship, In the famous battle between the *Brunswick* and the French *Vengeur de Peuple*, the two ships were so close together that the *Brunswick* could not open her gun-ports and had to blow them off! The *Vengeur* eventually sank.

By the evening victory was Howe's, but he was now too tired to exploit it. He had only napped in a chair since the French were sighted, and was now on the verge of collapse. The remainder of the French fleet was able to escape. More seriously, Howe was content with his victory and did not search for the grain ships, which escaped to France, saving the country.

CAPE ST. VINCENT

French Revolutionary War

Nelson and Jervis as Naval Tactician

1797

In 1797 Britain was desperately in need of a victory against all-conquering France and her allies. Britain was nearly bankrupt, allies had been lost, and the blockade of French and Dutch ports was being maintained with great difficulty. If the Spanish fleet came north and joined the French, the combination would be powerful enough to break the blockade. Admiral Sir John Jervis was ordered to keep watch to prevent the Spaniards making this move. So when he learnt that their fleet had left Cartagena with orders to make for Brest, he set out to intercept them, although his own fleet numbered only 14 against 27 enemy warships, Jervis' largest ship was the *Victory* and his smallest the *Diadem*, and every one of the Spanish ships was heavier and larger than its counterpart. The *Victory* was Jervis' flagship; Nelson, at this time, was a commodore and was sailing in the *Captain*.

On 14th February the Spaniards were sighted off Cape St. Vincent, Portugal. Jervis promptly noted that Spanish fleet was in two groups. He therefore sailed through the gap in between the two and attacked the section up wind. He realised that the other part of the Spanish fleet could not move up wind sufficiently quickly to help their fellows in the opening attack. British ships came up so fast and fire rapidly that the Spaniards were caught by surprise in the first broadside. As ship after ship came into action, it was obvious that the British were far superior in seamanship and gunnery. Even so, it was a close and fierce struggle. Jervis walked the deck unconcerned, even when a man was killed so close to him that Jervis was covered with his blood.

Nelson's task was to prevent the leeward section for joining the Spanish feet up wind. He attacked the four-decker *Santissima Trinidad* the largest ship in the world, which had 130 guns to his 74, and crippled her. Although his own ship was now a near-wreck, with no topsails, no wheel and sails to shreds, he then managed to board the *San Nicolas,* leading the assault party himself. Soon afterwards he led yet another boarding party, which captured the *San Josef*.

It was an astonishing victory and entirely due to excellent seamanship, accurate gunnery and bold, flexible naval tactics. Jervis was made an earl and Nelson was promoted to vice-admiral soon afterwards.

CAMPERDOWN

French Revolutionary War

Invasion of Ireland Repulsed

1797

Ireland was a favourite target for French intrigue during the Wars of the French Revolution, and in 1797, on the express urging of General Louis Lazare Hochem a force of 15,000 troops gathered in the area of the Texel in Holland to await a favourable opportunity to sail for Ireland in support of an Irish revolt. Amongst their number waited the exiled Irish revel, Wolfe Tone.

Although a suitable fleet was gathered, peculiarities of tide and wind kept the expedition in port. Only in October did a Dutch fleet of 16 small ships-of-the-line manage to put to sea, and it was hoped that the transports would soon follow them. News of the fleet's sailing was rapidly passed to England by a watchful Royal Navy frigate.

The year 1797 had been a critical one for the Royal Navy, seeing serious munities over living conditions at both Spithead and the Nore between

April and June. Admiral Adam Duncan was still not certain of the loyalty of all his crews when he set sail with 16 warships to seek out the fleet of Admiral Jan Willem de Winter.

On 11th October 1797, the British fleet caught sight of the Dutch vessels, and cleared for action. Although in numerical terms the fleets were equal, Duncan's ships were larger and carried a great many more guns than the Dutch. Duncan's secret fears about his men's loyalty soon evaporated, as they enthusiastically prepared for battle.

With the wind in their favour, the British bore down on their adversaries and went into thunderous action. Every effort was made to pass ships through the Dutch line, in order to cut off their possible line of retreat to the Dutch coast, which lay barely 10 miles distant. The individual ship-to-ship duels became intense, both fleets fighting with courage and determination. However, the superior destructive power of the heavier British broadsides soon began to tell.

At the end of the day, only seven Dutch ships made good their escape. The remaining nine, together with several frigates, fell into British hands. This victory, together with that won by Admiral John Jervis earlier in the year at Cape St Vincent, demonstrates the Royal' Navy's superiority at sea. To mark his victory, Admiral Duncan was made first a baron, and then Viscount Duncan of Camperdown.

NILE

French Revolutionary War

Nelson's Night Victory in Aboukir Bay

1798

On 8th May 1798 Rear-Admiral Horatio Nelson passed through the Straits of Gibraltar on a special mission, to find out both Napoleon's intentions, and where he was sending large consignments of arms. Napoleon was in fact preparing to mount an Eastern expedition to seize Egypt and advance on Persia. In so doing he would cut the British route to India.

Bad weather prevented Nelson from reaching Toulon before the French were away and converging on Malta, which they took and then sailed for Egypt. Nelson, reinforced to a total strength of 15 ships, switched this way and that, from Naples to Alexandria and Sicily, in a vain search. At last on 1st August his lookouts espied the battle fleet of Admiral Brueys anchored in Aboukir Bay. In the course of this mission Nelson had spent a great deal of time planning battle tactics with his captains, and he prepared to attack with a minimum of delay. At 1800 hours all was ready, but only two hours of daylight remained.

Admiral Brueys had 13 ships at anchor 200 metres apart in a shallow arc across the bay, and four frigates anchored inshore. Nelson sent his five leading ships through and round the van of the French line. Brueys had neglected to cover this flank with adequate onshore artillery. The British ships quickly chose their inshore positions, and began to blast the enemy. Nelson, following in *Vanguard*, led the rest of his fleet slowly along the French line on the seaward side, all guns thundering. Each British captain followed his orders to 'feel' for an opponent in the growing darkness. One by one the French ships fell under this two-sided taking fire. Brueys in the 120-gun *L'Orient* beat off and wrecked the 74-gun *Bellerophon*, only to encounter the guns of *Swiftsure* and *Alexander*, which attacked on both quarters. Brueys was cut in two by a shot, and at about 2200 the ship blew up with an awe-inspiring roar.

Battle continued through the night, and at dawn Admiral Villeneuve escaped with the French remnant of two ships of the line and two frigates. With this one terrible blow Nelson wrecked Napoleon's Eastern expedition, cutting off the French army in Egypt.

Napoleon was to escape and return to France, but his nation had suffered a most severe blow to its pride and morale.

ACRE

French Revolutionary War

A Repulse for General Bonaparte

1799

Cut off from France after the Battle of the Nile, General Bonaparte determined to forestall a Turkish invasion of Egypt by invading Syria in early 1799. Despite an outbreak of plaque in the army and a delay at El Arish, the campaign proceeded well enough. Jaffa was captured and the French advance proceeded through what is today Israel, until the town of Acre was reached. Standing on a small peninsula jutting into the Mediterranean, 'the key of Palestine' was held by the fanatical Djezzar-Pasha and his Moslem troops, aided by a Royal Navy squadron of two vessels commanded by Sir Commodore William Sidney Smith. On board was his friend, the French émigré Colonel Phelypeaux, who had studied at the Ecole Militaire in Paris and was a skilled engineer.

On 18th March 1799 the French settled down to besiege Acre, but the Royal Navy had already complicated the problem for them by capturing the heavy siege guns travelling from Egypt by sea. Deprived of a siege train and so short of ammunition that Bonaparte had to offer a reward for the recovery of enemy cannon balls, the French had recourse to a series of eight attempts at an assault – but each was beaten back in turn. Commodore Smith landed guns from his ships, and a strong force of seamen to strengthen the resolve of Djezzar-Pasha, whilst Phelypeaux constructed field-works to strengthen the out-dated fortifications of the town. Even more important, the Royal Navy was able to assure the arrival of fresh supplies for the garrison by sea – and to deprive the French besiegers of succour from the same source. So the weeks dragged on into months.

Meanwhile a large Turkish army was assembling at Damascus, and in mid-siege Bonaparte had to lead off a force of 2,500 men from Acre to rescue General Kleber outnumbered covering force. The result was the Battle of Mount Tabor (16th April) where the French routed a reputed 35,000 Turks. Returning to Acre, Bonaparte resumed command of the siege, but all his drive and will-power could not achieve the impossible. The British naval presence was indubitably the critical factor, for the ships were to enfilade the French approach trenches, as well as to provide men and munitions to strengthen the defence. With plague decimating his ranks, Bonaparte was finally forced to concede defeat.

COPENHAGEN

French Revolutionary War

An Audacious Victory for Nelson

1801

In the darkest days of the Napoleonic Wars (1793-1815), Britain stood alone against the forces of the revolutionary French republic under its imperialist general, Napoleon Bonaparte. Isolated by the victorious French and denied essential raw materials by an alliance: 'the Armed Neutrality', of former allies, Britain's life sustaining commerce was threatened.

Fortunately Britain could boast a great and original naval commander in Horatio Nelson, who had lost an eye in 1794 fighting in Corsica and his right arm three years later while assaulting Teneriffe.

In 1801 serving as vice-admiral to Sir Hyde Park, Nelson conceived an audacious plan to defeat the Danish, whose defence of the west bank of the Sound running for 25 miles north-south between Denmark and Sweden seemed invincible. Guns bristled from the forts of Elsinore (Hamlet's castle) and Cronenberg, which was guarded by Fort Trekroner. Ranged in front of the city defences was the whole Danish fleet, mustering 628 guns. In the Sound itself, unmarked by buoys, lay deadly shallows to trap the invader.

The British fleet avoided the batteries of Elsinore and Cronenberg by hugging the Swedish coast. Nelson then split off his force of 12 line-of-battle ships and 17 smaller vessels from Parker's fleet and used the wind to sail to a position below the large sandbank in the middle of the Sound. Once there, he prayed for the wind to change. It did so and enabled Nelson to sail next morning up the other edge of the shallows and engage the Danish line in furious cannon barrage. The Danes exchanged shot for shot for two hours.

Admiral Parker, seeing from afar that no headway was being made, signalled Nelson by flag 'Discontinue the Action'. Nelson put his telescope to his blind eye, declaring: 'I have only one eye; I have a right to be blind sometimes'. Disregarding the signal, he urged his men to greater efforts. They responded nobly and valiantly.

With the battle still raging, Nelson claimed victory, outbluffing the Danish prince, who called a truce. In the action the Danes lost 17 out of 18 ships and 6,000 men were killed or wounded, compared to 1,000 British casualties. Nelson defeated the Danish so soundly that Britain was again able to obtain supplies of hemp, wood and pitch from the Baltic, without which Britain's navy would have collapased.

ASSAYE AND ARGAUM

Second Anglo-Maratha War

Wellesley Conquers Central India

1803

As British influence spread over India, opposition was encountered from the Princes of Scindia and Berar, and the Mahratta people, and this the French were not slow to exploit.

To tackle the Mahratta problem, the Governor-General of India, Lord Mornington, despatched two armies, one (13,500 men and 22 guns strong) commanded by his brother. Major General Arthur Wellesley. After six weeks marching, Wellesley encountered the enemy, 90.000 strong (including 20,000 Mahratta cavalry and 98 cannons), drawn up between the Rivers Kaitna and Juah near Assaye on 23rd September 1803. Despite the unfavourable odds and the strong position, Wellesley decided to attack. Whilst his cavalry watched the enemy horsemen, he moved his infantry and guns over an unmarked ford to turn the enemy's left, only to discover that the Princes had realigned their forces to face East. This compelled

Wellesley to advance against the enemy guns, commanded by a skilled German mercenary, Pohlmann. Using his only British Regiments, the 74th, as his spearhead, he pressed home his attack with five battalions in oblique order, despite the uncertain morale of his sepoys. Overrunning the gun-line, he wheeled his formations to assault the defences protecting Assaye.

General Maxwell and the British 19th Dragoons defeated a counter-attack by Berar's horsemen on a British right, and a strong infantry attack over-whelmed the defenders of Assaye. By 6 pm Wellesley had inflicted 6,000 casualties and suffered only 1,600.

Wellesley next undertook the invasion of Berar, but despite reinforcement by Colonel Stevenson he could muster barely 10,000 men. Once again, however, he advanced boldly against the Sultan, whose army he dis-covered on 29th November strongly entrenched with 39 guns around the town of Argaum. The first attack was repulsed by accurate fire, but after rallying his shaken sepoys Wellesley led a second onslaught at 4.30 pm. Whilst Stevenson cavalry fought off the Scindian horsemen on the left, and Wellesley's own cavalry routed the Berar horsemen on the right, his infan-try swarmed over the defences to split the enemy centre. For a loss of 46 killed and 315 wounded, Wellesley had inflicted 5,000 casualties and cap-tured all the Berar guns.

This success brought the Second Mahratta War to a victorious conclusion.

TRAFALGAR

Napoleonic War

Nelson's Greatest Victory

1805

The Campaign

In 1805 Britain faced one of the most serious threats in her history. France and Spain were allied against her, controlling most of the Atlantic and Mediterranean coasts of Europe. At Boulogne Napoleon had assembled the Grand Army and a fleet of invasion transports. However, these could not cross the Channel without being destroyed by the British squadrons in the Straits of Dover. All the French and Spanish fleets were far away, blockaded in their bases by British ships. Napoleon's plan for breaking this stalemate was for the French and Spanish fleets to slip out of their bases at Brest, Ferrol, Toulon and Cadiz under cover of darkness or bad weather. The combined fleets would assemble in the West Indies and then, while the British were still searching for them, return and overwhelm the British forces in the Channel. This would secure the passage of the invasion troops and once they were ashore in Britain, Napoleon had no doubt that the war would soon be over.

However brilliant it looked on paper this plan took no account of the difficulties of moving fleets of sailing ships, dependent on wind, weather and tide. This was shown as soon as the French Mediterranean Fleet, under Admiral Villeneuve, escaped from Toulon in January. They immediately met a gale which caused so much damage that they were forced back to port. After repairs Villeneuve sailed again on 31st March, picked up some Spanish ships at Cadiz and reached Martinique in the West Indies on 14th May. He was pursued by the British Mediterranean Fleet under Lord Nelson which unfortunately had to struggle against the wind, taking a month to reach Gibraltar, a voyage which took Villeneuve only nine days. However, Nelson had better luck with the Atlantic winds and reached Barbados on 4th June, Had he not been misled by false information, Nelson might have caught up with Villeneuve fleet then.

Meanwhile Napoleon's other squadrons had been unable to escape and when he heard the news of Nelson's arrival Villeneuve hurried back to Europe. On 22nd July he met a British fleet which was waiting for him off Cape Finisterre and an indecisive engagement was fought in a thick sea mist. He joined the squadron in Ferrol, but the British squadrons, including Nelson's, were now concentrating off Ushant. This meant that Napoleon's plan had failed; far from being dispersed over the oceans, the British fleet was concentrated between his own squadrons and the invasion army. Villeneuve made a half-hearted effort to break out in mid-August but despaired and ran to Cadiz, where he was quickly blockaded. This ended the invasion attempt; on 29th August the Grand Army broke camp and marched against the Austrians. However, Villeneuve's fleet was still a powerful force and after a short stay in England, Nelson was sent to command the blockading force.

Nelson's Pan

Napoleon now ordered the Cadiz Fleet to return to the Mediterranean to assist the campaign in Italy. Villeneuve sailed from Cadiz on 20th October with 34 ships of the line. He was shadowed by British frigates and on 21st October Nelson, with 27 ships, found him off Cape Trafalgar, between Cadiz and Gibraltar. The combined French and Spanish fleets straggled into a long line as it approached almost at right angles in two untidy lines. Nelson was determined to force a decisive battle and had earlier discussed his plans in detail with his captains. One division of 14 ships under Collingwood was to concentrate on the rear of the enemy line, while Nelson would lead his line of 13 ships to threaten the enemy's leading ships and then strike at the centre. This would prevent the leaders from helping the rear until it was too late. To protect the two lines during the long approach Nelson placed his strongest ships, such as his own flagship, *Victory*, at the head of the lines.

The Battle Begins

As the British fleet came in sight, the Combined Fleet turned towards Cadiz, but a battle was now inevitable. On board the British ships the men ate an early dinner of salt pork and biscuit. At 11:40 Nelson made his famous signal 'England expects that every man this day will do his duty', followed by his last signal, 'Engage the enemy more closely'. Just before noon the enemy opened fire on Collingwood's flagship, the *Royal Sovereign*. At 12:08 *Royal Sovereign* replied with a double-shotted broadside which caused nearly 400 casualties. For nearly 15 minutes she was the only English ship action. The rest of Collingwood's Fleet was soon hidden in clouds of powder smoke.

The Main Action

At 12:30 *Victory* broke through the enemy line, firing a treble-shotted broadside into the stern windows of Villeneuve's flagship, the *Bucentaure*. This broadside crippled *Bucentaure* and the *Victory* moved on to engage the *Redoubtable*. The two ships were soon locked together and the *Victory's* deck came under sweeping fire from marksmen in the fighting-tops on the masts of the French ship. One shot hit Nelson in the left shoulder and lodged against his spine. He was carried below, but the surgeon could do nothing to save his Admiral.

The battle was now at its height in the centre and rear. Nelson's skilful tactics and the superior gunnery and training of the British fleet began to tell. The *Redoubtable* had 491 killed and 81 wounded out of 600 men; two other French ships had over 500 casualties each. (The *Victory's* casualties, 57 dead were the highest in the British fleet). Within two hours the centre and rear of the Combined Fleet had effectively been defeated and the battle began to die down as ships struck their colours. At about three o'clock the 10 ships of the van squadron made a belated appearance, but they were kept away from their hard-pressed comrades by an improvised line of British ships. In this phase of action three French ships were dismasted and forced to surrender. The battle ended in a disjointed series of fights as the remnants of the French and Spanish fleets struggled to break away to Cadiz and the British tried to secure their prizes before nightfall. The last shots were fired about 4.30 pm. The French ship *Achille* was on fire and burnt until she blew up about an hour later.

The Death of Nelson

Meanwhile Nelson was dying abroad the *Victory*, his last hours distracted by the noise of the ships broadsides. Although in great pain he continued to follow the course of the battle and knew that he had won a great victory. Sensing that a storm was likely in the night, he ordered his flag captain, Thomas Hardy, to signal the fleet to anchor. He grew gradually weaker and died at 4.30 pm.

The Results of The Battle

Trafalgar was the most crushing victory of the sailing ship era and a fitting climax to Nelson's career. Eighteen enemy ships were captured or sunk, and four of the remainder were captured on 4th November. The survivors never again ventured out from Cadiz. During the storm which followed the battle, three of the surrendered ships were recaptured and only four others survived the storm, although many were severely battered.

In the fleet and in England rejoicing over the victory was tempered by grief at Nelson's death. His body was brought back to England preserved in a barrel of brandy and given a State Funeral in St Paul's Cathedral. Villeneuve was less fortunate. He survived the battle, but committed suicide on his way to Paris rather than face Napoleon's anger.

Although the Napoleonic Wars continued for 10 years after Trafalgar the French navy was never again in a position to challenge British maritime supremacy. Trafalgar was the beginning of that period of Pax Britannica which was last until 1914.

Printed in Great Britain
by Amazon

17539934R00079